BORN IN THE YEAR OF THE BUTTERFLY KNIFE

BORN IN THE YEAR OF THE BUTTERFLY KNIFE

DERRICK C. BROWN

Write Bloody Publishing ©2006

SPECIAL THANKS FOR HELPING THIS BOOK COME TOGETHER:

Thom Meredith

Claude Le Monde

Jeff McDaniel

Joel Chmara

Buddy Wakefield

Blaine Fontana

Leigh White

Paul Suntup

Matt Carver

Tank Farm

Carolin Matzko

Aimee Bender

Marc Smith

Taylor Mali

Eitan Kadosh

Mike McGee

Tim Ellis

Krystal Ashe

Tatiana Simonian

Buddy Wakefield

Amarillo

Amanda Valentine

Matt Maust

Open Bookstore

Stephen Latty

AUTHOR'S NOTE

BORN IN THE YEAR OF THE BUTTERFLY KNIFE

Here it is. Twelve years of writing. Ten years of reading and touring. Opera Houses, theaters, churches, coffee shops, restaurants, garages and bars, all over the world, all breathed out from these books. These poems were selected by myself, so I wouldn't have to reprint the old texts, since many of the past publishers are out of business. Poetry is a tough racket, the bastard child of the arts. But I am so thankful for diving into this art form. The life I have seen because of it has been raw and remarkable. The people I owe are endless. Fistfights in coffee shops, seeing your poems tattooed on people, crying with old men after a reading, people sharing their inspiration over absinthe or beer, all this is the impetus that keeps me going. It certainly isn't the cash or helicopter booty. After re-reading many of these texts I find that many themes keep occurring: dogs, God, riots, knives, blood, death and women. Great. I hope you enjoy the new work; feel free to ignore my commentary and forgive me if I've ever screwed you over. I'm trying to do better. Please read this book in public.

Enjoy the dusk.

D.

SELECTIONS TAKEN FROM THESE BOOKS:

"Born In The Year Of The Butterfly Knife" 2004 Write Bloody Publishing
"Unapologetics" (Prose) (Out of print)
"I'm Easier Said Than Done" 2003 (Out of print)
"If Lovin' You Is Wrong, Then I Don't Want To Be Wrong" 2001 Moodorgandistro
"Junebug Melatonin" 2000 KAPOW Books
"The Joy Motel" 1998 (Out of print)
"Hostile Pentecostal" (Pre-released as *"Upside Brown"*) 1995 (Hopefully out of print)

FOR INFO, WRITEBLOODY@BROWNPOETRY.COM.
BOOK LAYOUT AND FRONT COVER - MATT MAUST - COLDWARKIDS.COM
PAINTINGS - BLAINE FONTANA (MIXED MEDIA ON PLYWOOD) - TOTEMBOOKMEDIA.COM
ILLUSTRATIONS - MATT CARVER (INK AND MOUNTAIN DEW ON NOTEBOOK PAPER) - MATTCARVER@GMAIL.COM

HIRE THEM.

I could never give you all the daylight you wanted
but here's some of the dusk you need.

— Derrick C. Brown

The massive acceptance and love you
poured upon this weirdo saved me,

For Nancy Counts

BORN IN THE YEAR OF THE BUTTERFLY KNIFE

BORN IN THE YEAR OF THE BUTTERFLY KNIFE

THE KUROSAWA CHAMPAGNE

This poem was built after watching Kurosawa's Dreams and The Lady from Shanghai by Orson Welles. It is infused with a time I watched a lover have a nightmare and did not wake her.

THE KUROSAWA CHAMPAGNE MAQUET.

Tonight
your body shook,
hurling your nightmares
back to Cambodia.

Your nightgown wisped off
into Ursula Minor.

I was left here on earth feeling alone,
paranoid about the Rapture.

Tonight
I think it is safe to say we drank too much.
Must I apologize for the volume in my slobber?
Must I apologize for the best dance moves ever?
No.

Booze is my tuition to clown college.

I swung at your purse.
It was staring at me.

We swerved home on black laughter.
bleeding from forgettable boxing.

I asked you to sleep in the shape of a trench
so that I might know shelter.

I drew the word surrender in the mist of your breath,
waving a white sheet around your body.

'Dear, in the morning let me put on your make-up for you.
I'll be loading your gems with mascara
then I'll tell you the truth...'
I watched black ropes and tears ramble down your face.

Lady war paint.

A squad of tiny men rappels down those snaking lines
and you say;
"Thank you for releasing all those fuckers from my life."

You have a daily pill case.
There are no pills inside.
It holds the ashes of people who died
...the moment they saw you.

The cinema we built was to play the greats
but we could never afford the power
so in the dark cinema
you painted pictures of Kurosawa.

I just stared at you like Orson Welles,
getting fat off your style.

You are a movie that keeps exploding.
You are Dante's fireplace.

We were so broke,
I'd pour tap water into your mouth,
burp against your lips
so you could have champagne.

You love champagne.

Sparring in the candlelight.

Listen—
the mathematical equivalent of a woman's beauty
is directly relational
to the amount or degree
other women hate her.

You, dear, are hated.

Your boots are a soundtrack to adultery.
Thank God your feet fall in the rhythm of loyalty.

If this kills me,
slice me julienne
uncurl my veins
and fashion yourself a noose
so I can hold you
once more.

THE CHINESE ELEVATOR

Sometimes you can feel them in love somewhere else in the city and it is like having a phantom limb.

He is staring at a bottle of pills big as a lamp.
Brighter.

He sighs a noise that comes in the sounds of ripped silks.

He loves the steady drums of her headboard
played by a stranger.

It is the tempo and timbre of men
slicing the earth with shovels.

He loves knowing that she can't last a season
without a new salesman knocking at her heart
through her uterus.

His record player has laryngitis.

The telephone's tongue has been cut out.

He had linked his heartbeat with hers.
Now apart, when her blood races
so does his.

At least he finally removed the saddle
from his head.

Someone fair had straddled his skull,
rode his dreams into the ground.

He lies still in bed with his pulse, now rising
touching his fingers to the sound.

A mouth opens nervously and dry
like young prom legs.

'I still want you.'

...but the woman is far and pregnant
with blood.

The blood is due.

He removes his medical bracelet. It reads:
'I left my heart in someone's veins.
She bleeds Valentines once a month.'

She was born with backwards guts.
Waltzing was miserable.
Always spinning. Leading with her spine.
Keeping her heart behind her.

He is a Little Boy who has fallen
over some Nagasaki.

Lovers are on stage at the comedy club.
He is a heckler who can only sob into a bullhorn.

Love is a bullet that crawls on all fours
He stumbles in the night to the poetry of whores.

Exhausted, dirty and loose.

Piss of a fighter.
Shit as a lover.
The box he checks is other.
He has the handwriting of his Mother.
The vanishing act of his Father.

'We bury this now'
is muttered
as she unrobes
for a shiny new lover.

Across town he sits up in bed
says.
'You bring the dirt,
I'll bring the shovels.
You warn the heavens.
I'll tell the others.'

He had grown tired of pressing his head
to his lover's chest
only to hear the sound of
children gasping.

It was her favorite love song.
in harmony with the creaking of dark robots inside her.

Our bed squeaked out a bad musical.

He subscribes to the newspaper,
looks for the black stilts of her name
in the obituaries.

Hangs his countenance on the wall,
crawls into bed
with a handful of pills to cancel everything.

He simply rode the Chinese elevator.
Pushed the wrong button.

Someone went all the way down.

PUNISH CHILDREN

If I ever have a kid, they'll probably be a spaz to pay me back for my brazenness.

Who will curl forth honesty
and say that they would like to send their child back
to that sudden baby cave?

I fear having a boy
fore seeing the day I will stare into his skin
and have to say:
"You might unravel, son.
Do not try to prepare for this.
Know that I don't know shit. No one does."

I fear having a girl the most,
who will ask me what it's like to die
and I will have to reply:

"Lose your virginity
and fall asleep in pain.
Be better than me."

If that small, hairless, voteless tyrant says:

            "Stop talking like you're trying, Pop.
What is it really like to die?
Speak plain."

I will say:
            "Love writing with all your heart.
Then have kids
and write no more,
you wretched, screeching Leprechaun."

She has that laugh 'cause she has my sense of humor.
How strange that the woman you always wanted to meet
came out of your own body.

How egotistical and pure.

My past rushes through her like a river after winter.

I hope she fails history.

WALTZING THE HURRICANE

If women only knew how dyslexic they can turn men by only holding their gaze on them for a few extra seconds.

Waterslide architects have been spying
the smooth of your back,

Mapping blueprints
from the finger trails
adoring up your spine

stealing your design.

Do not keep ask me for more revelations, dear
or I will just keep sending you to the back of the Bible.

Revelation 12:7
And there was war in heaven.

It's still there.

In this light
I can see through your body.

Black Hills Indians wrapped your bones in arrows and feathers
for the day you make your exit, inspiring new battles in heaven.

Enemies sliced by the wit in your lipstick.

You are a Sunday porch I could do nothing on
and feel like everything was happening.

Let me pull my hurricane move—
a move to turn your gilded fortress to shrapnel—
to windscorch your overbooked rickshaws,
melting your slippers into glass formula.
Girling you out.
Bursting your leggings
into pink shredded wheat.

AAAAAAH!

Andromeda Carnivora
envy of novas
zing your flesh across twilight.

Stay asleep
so the aircraft aren't drawn to land
on the Christmas lights
crackling safety signals
from your eyes.

I saw you
panting in the oven of your skin.

Aren't you tired of awakening next to lost armies?
Sick of people looking for jade in your nostrils?

Subterranean teeth-gnashing orchestra.
Zebra killer.
Flexed duchess.
Carved cha-cha-cha.
Zirconia sass rock.

I want the theater without the drama.
I want the opera without the soap.

Lay in the stillness of a fighting-saints fairy tale.

Your partner is here,
a frog in a coma of kisses.
You, dressed as wonder,
screwed me backwards
with your
dyslexic kiss.

Fairytale saints fighting a stillness.
Kisses of coma.
Here is partner your.
Wonder dressed you.
Backwards me screwed.
Kiss dyslexic.   **19**

THE SILENT FALL OF NEW YORK CITY

Beau Sia, Jason Muhlberger, Rob Neil, Cristin Okeefe Aptowicz and I experienced a real NYC blizzard and I've never heard the city silenced before. It was the most beautiful time with fantastic people. I couldn't stop laughing and no one was saying anything.

New York City fought the quiet for too long.

Taxis poking through the white
like Corn Pops in cold milk.

A sneak attack of slow down.

It came to us
the way a kiss turns into
a sudden veil.

The blizzard has sent down a bride.

THE DAWN OF WEIRD

This is the first and maybe last time I will use the word 'Twas. I don't know why I have these visions, but I do.

AT GAURD AT THE HUMAN GARDEN

Twas the dawn of Weird
and I had woken up early.

There was no difference between
sky and sea,
so dogs chased tennis balls into the shore break
of cumulus clouds.

Sea lions flew point
in the formations of sparrows.
Fishermen caught birds,
apologized
and set them free.
The birds were understanding and as a gift
brought back worm sandwiches
which were surprisingly tasty.

Airplanes landed safely underwater
as mermaids guided us in with pop-electric jellyfish.

Guns had turned to black licorice.
All the cops were nibbling on shotguns
and one by one all the criminals cried
and turned themselves in
to the dentist.

Hospitals morphed and became
rubber bounce castles.
They had to call security
to usher out the scalpels
and to keep the elderly
from hogging the twisty slide.

Billboards became drive-in movie screens
replaying what our feet looked like
when we were chasing our dreams.

Everyone walked home.

And all the tombstones
in all the graveyards
crumbled into seeds.

Flora bloomed immediately.

Bees halted on the outskirts
of the cemetery walls,
reverence for the ending,
the passing of all.

With antennae bowed
and honey tears starting,
they pledged to stand guard
of the bright human garden.

The largest pile of flowers...
It rose from your name.
The wind swelled a whisper
That said

They're O.K., they're all O.K.'

My Lord, it was a solid mountain of sunflowers.

The world blazed in color and I welcomed the change.
It was the dawn of weird and the morning of strange.

Amazing how all this
did come to pass,
just a child cutting loose
in a poetry class.

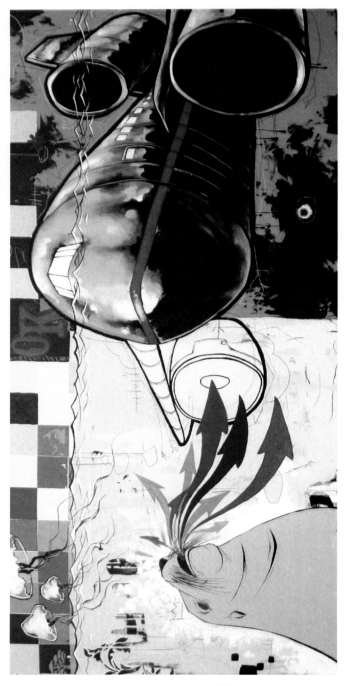

WITH THE GUIDANCE OF DOLPHINS

If you write, the dark spots can be considered the sweet spots.

I found the coordinates for the payphone that rests
at the bottom of the Pacific
near the Channel Islands.

Soon you will get a call from me.
You will know in your stomach
before you answer.

I am binding barbells to my boots
for the stroll to the lightless floor.

Change in one fist.
A zip-lock bag of air in the other...

I stand at the shore and stomp on the sand 5 times.
Blind bottlenose dolphins arrive—
guide me in slow like secret service.
They had done this before.

30 feet down
My head feels like it will explode
as it did whenever I saw a typewriter.

I dwell on the idea of who started the fires in hell.
Who built such a place?
I understand that it wasn't the devil.

My arms lift unto him.

There are things we don't talk about
that can only be talked about on this payphone.
Now in front of me:

The damage in our foreheads-
The hands cut off for stealing ideas-
The hearts donated to lost and found and lost-
The empty,
like the way you kissed me goodnight
after your second abortion.

Love, your phone is ringing.

HOW TO FEEL

I find myself screaming out loud in futility at the television, like a guy watching sports telling the coach what to do. The only difference is I am watching the news or things like this.

'It's not looking too good, but he is alive.'

Kid is bleeding all over doctors.
A family is crying on a reality show called Shock Trauma.

Son has been in a car wreck.
Disconnected his head
from his spine.

After a commercial break, Dr. Cooper meets with the family.

'It's not looking too good, but he is alive.'

Dad says 'Thank you for your candor. He...He's very important to us...'
and breaks down.

The doctor says 'I understand' and leaves.

The camera stays for the weeping.
No one tells the camera to turn off.

My leg hits the remote.
The next channel has a beautiful woman offering me something.

The perfection said to me
'What do you want?'

I said I wanted what all guys want:

to smack the beauty back into you
with a light bulb revolver,
to call down fire from the holy spirit
and watch you incinerate in a cheap party gown,
to rip you in two and make you notice
how close we are to death when sleeping,
to awaken that four-letter beast
roaring like a fistfight in your throat
that unsleeps the chaos inside you.

I want you to become one of us,
a clumsy feisty anti-zombie,
hungry for that famous arrow,
pounding at confusing walls
like a foreigner at the gates, ya know?

A boy was bleeding on another channel.

I had forgotten all about him.

TO THE LIGHTNING TEACHERS

All this you are holding is because someone said something encouraging to me once.

PEARLS, PORCUPINES, PENNIES

To the teacher that said
'The world is your oyster...'
These poems are the pearls
I spit upon your plate.

To the other teachers,
prepare your flints.
Speak with the hum of Fahrenheit
in your hearts.

Teach them to be artists.
Teach them that artists make people aware
of what they already know
and really know
what they themselves think they don't know.

Teach the champions the necessity of losing
for the sake of personality.

If the kids are hard to reach
wearing jackets made of knives,
maybe it's time that we
dressed up like porcupines
to show there's a bit of them
still poking inside us.

Hey you prickly mother!
The kid under your bed is dying every day.
Dying to play in the mud, dying to snap all your friggin' pencils,
dying to understand fireflies in the tree line.

Go get them, teachers.
We should all be lighting kids on fire
unless you are a literalist,
or are from Salem.

Bring them an astral storm of ideas.

Lightning strikes the tree-
the tree is budding with pinecones-
the pinecones explode-
the seed spreads across the forest-
new trees are born.

Bring them the lightning.
Bring them the sauce.

I was a bag of dirty pennies from the year 73
and a teacher, Mrs. Shin, rolled me around in hot sauce till I was clean.
She knew I wasn't the Ivy League type, but she still brought ignition.
"Oh, you all went to the school of business—
I went to the school of none of your business.
I'm different."

She taught me that the word is dangerous.
It's good to look a dream in the eyeball and not look away.
It's good to have a voice that can speak the language of resuscitation.
It's good to be beat down like the sun to prove you can rise.

The future is our youth dressed as roman candles
ready to burst open the gray evening sky.

12 pens in a bandolier!

A vending machine on campus full of envelopes
addressed to the White House!

A megaphone inside each lunch pail!

Tell kids everywhere—
The world is your underwear.

It's time you changed it.

BLOOD TEST

Where do you go when you go to your head world?
My quiet head scares the crap outta me most nights.

At 10:35pm I got real quiet inside
like you said I should.

I shook like a dog in a cage,
trying to run from the sound of fireworks.

Hungry for the language that could make you know this.

Terribles were forming in the place where the tongue
grows out of the neck.

I went inside.

It sounded like tunnels exploding.

I'm not sure if I came out.

HOT FOR SORROW

This is my favorite ballad. In Munich, I met the kids from a mesmerizing group called Broken Social Scene. I asked if they would let me use their music when I do this out loud. They are gracious people and they are Canadian. The poetic terrorism guys use lines from this one when tagging up places. God bless 'em.

When the police helicopters showed up
I grabbed onto the skid
and they flew me cross town
to your house.
I watched you through the glass as you slept

like jewelry in a coffin.

I screamed out

"Hey!

I don't want to be the best lover you've ever had
I just want to be your favorite."

File me under hot for sorrow.

When I couldn't find your picture, I ate unwanted videotape and dreamt.
When you appeared, soft-focused,
outlined in lasers,
embarrassed of your little T-Rex arms and seaweed hair,
we danced on the ceiling like Lionel Richie
until it was time to walk you home
from naked class.

This crosseyed sniper
misses you so much.

The heavy solo night music
tells me what is buried beneath our city:

Ambulances hooked on one ballad-
A sky turning red over its opponents.

Night melodies of helicopter switchblades
slice through this city.

The noise tells me there is still crime down there.
5000 air machines cannot stop crime.
5000 searchlights cannot stop crime.
5000 police fully moustached, with a John Wayne box-set,
and our names on every baton
cannot stop crime.

I now know that what I feel for you is crime.

This is why I like the sound of police choppers:
not because it makes me feel safe and watched over
but rather because it is the music of war,

and tonight
they were playing our war.

ARMSTRONG

This poem became a song. I love telescopes. I never know what I'm looking at, but I could stare all night and imagine scenes happening 14 billion light years away.

For Mike Mcgee

The night the moon cracked open
A voice came from within.

The moon turned to the astronaut
and said to him
'Please stay. Please stay.'

The astronaut looked
back at the moon

said "I'd love to stay
but I can't stay with you

I am sorry to report

that I must leave.

For when I'm here

with you

I cannot breathe."

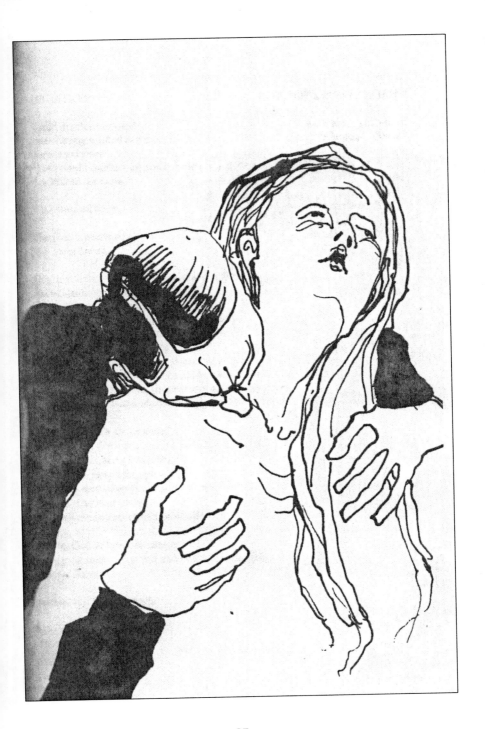

MEDUSA OBLONGATA

Get mad on paper. Then become human. Toss this in the revenge pile.

I wished for you like old women wished they would've perished first.

Every kiss was a dead language.

Every kiss was a chance to spit in your mouth.

Now you let your skirt fall like an empire.

Lead his tongue into the Nile.

Taste the meat around his teeth.

Promote his hands from your jowls to your breasts.

As he beats the snakes out of you—

Your spot turns to soup.

Drown him in this month's blood.

No matter how hard you drill,

Brother, you will not find oil.

Feel her sex go tepid.

Non-seduced spasmo-cadavers.

Pretend I no longer dwell in you.

I told you I'd return.

I am in his medicated thrust.

I am in his wallet as it buys your legs into the air.

I am his hiss crawling across your tonsils.

Call it a night.

Call it what it is.

When I said you were remarkable

I said real marketable.

Some churches are abandoned

but can't be torn down.

You are smoke.

COME ALIVE

Some days I feel so damn good, I want to take you with me.

COME ALIVE MR. TRUFALUMP

Citizens of Narnia:
I must admit
I was a reluctant candidate for Mayor.

I have shaken the hands and hooves of many
through out this great land

And I must admit
for many, the beat inside has died.

A great sorrow overwhelms me
for even the drums in my chest
are growing quieter each day.

When did we become a library of children,
shelved like great novels
no one had time to read?

As Mayor of Narnia
I declare that this day must be the day we come alive.
I will declare a day for dipping our hands in butter
so we can practice letting go of what we were
and watch our hands emerge as telephones
so we can know our true calling.

Brrrrrng. It's for you. It's the future!

As Mayor of Narnia,
I will declare a day of common sense
on behalf of waiters everywhere.
If you can't tip 15-20%
then you don't get to go out to eat.

As Mayor of Narnia
I declare a day for talking to the trees.

What are they saying? They're saying 'Climb me,
carve your future lover's initials into my spine,
sacrifice me for your books.
Every book, every page is my blood. I give this to you.
If it's a war for the lands of imagination, I am ready to die.'

They're saying,
Go ahead-get young as your brain thinks you are on this day.

Invite snow angels to a bonfire
and give them s'more-flavored popsicles.

Buy cereal with the worst nutritional value
but the biggest prize.
Go meet your prize.

Sing and misplace your keys.

See yourself dressing as a bull, waiting in Spanish arenas,
armed with a journal and some pointy horns
rising from all fours
chasing matadors
and screaming,
'Chapter 1! I was born for this! Now how do you like it, Sucka!

We're gonna fly kites in reverse
with the sail planted firmly in the soil
and our bodies on a string
sculpting clouds into the faces of people we miss.

We're gonna make thank-you cards
and rest them on soldiers' graves.

We're gonna raise a hand
in the back of the world classroom
and the answer we come up with
is to pull the night down
stare stars in the face
and reclaim lost wishes.

We're gonna capture the details.
We're gonna turn off the machines.

We are not the dishes we pass.
We are the passion we dish.

If you've been away from Narnia for a while, welcome back.

The kingdom is outside.
The kingdom is inside.
Today is the day we come alive.

from **UNAPOLOGETICS**

THE LABRADOR IS POSED IN THE FREEZER

Linda could not look the panting German Shepherd in the face.

It was shaking like a young actor.

Dogs shake at the veterinarian not because they are scared to die,
but because they are scared to leave their master. Even if it's just a
check-up, dogs smell death as well as they smell fear and for Zinger, the pink
smell had become strong.

Small room with doctor.

Technician enters with guest. Customer folds her lips
back into her mouth and clutches her car keys, sets her purse upon the hairy,
scratched tile.

Linda the technician holds the animal in the aggressive posture, pinned like a
Greco champion.

Shove forearm along back. Headlock. Hold down back legs with left hand. Do
not look the dog in the face. Customer is crying like she is drowning. Shaking
her head at this scene she never imagined.

Dog is pinned on counter atop of green beach towel 'cause of shit and piss.

"Would you like to say something, Ma'm?"

"Oh God. Jesus. Jesus Christ. Baby, I'm sorry. I'm sorry I couldn't...Aw jeez. I
just couldn't afford the surgery. Maybe...a...took a double shift or more hours
so...so...I could...Jesus Christ."

"Ma'm?"

Breathing, breathing, house-key-hitting-car-key sounds. The dog is trying to
lunge but is too old to overpower Linda. The woman stands up, hand on hip
and taps her foot nervously, takes a deep breath as if to ready herself for a
blow to the ribs, touches the dog on the forehead and said in a soft collected
tone:
"O.K."

Linda the technician can't help but look towards the back of the head of the Shepherd. Its face tilts toward the owner. There is a whimper and its sharp ears perk up. Not to say help me. Not to say I'm scared. It says:

"Why? Why?"

Linda sees the Shepherd's eyes. Linda cries and buries her face in the fabric softener smell of her lab coat.

The customer repeats "O.K." and the stops fidgeting.
Still panting with its tongue out.
The pink death is inserted into the artery near the leg. It's so efficient, seconds.

The Shepherd is gone. There is piss.

Ten minutes alone are granted and the woman, the customer,
falls over the shell of her animal.

In the hallway outside the small room, Dr. Matzko turns to Linda.

"You cry every time now."

"I can't help but look, doctor. I'm sorry. The eyes are getting me lately."

"The eyes of Zinger or the eyes of Mrs. Walters?"

"I go in there feeling strong as an ox. Then something happens where I just feel so much for these animals, I imagine hanging onto that moment. Once they're gone, I can treat their carcasses like sleeping bags and it doesn't faze me. That table, the needle and everything lately...
I think I can handle it and then something hits that trigger."

"I was like you in school, Linda. That's why I hired you. You've got a great heart for animals. Scott may be more composed, but I like your heart. The only thing I wonder about is that you seemed to have a better grip on yourself a few months ago."

"It's just a freak thing. I know it's unprofessional and I promise I'll get control of my emotions next time. Once again, I apologize."

There is still sobbing coming from Mrs. Walker in the small room.

With permission from Dr. Matzko, Linda goes home early, eats ice cream,
naps in a weird fetal position on her couch and returns several hours later for
the night shift with fellow intern Scott Hornsby. When the long hours drag into
the A.M.,
Linda pulls down her keyboard from the bird food cabinet and jams although
she is never actually
playing it. She always just hits the demo button and moves her fingers across t
he keys.
There is a harpsichord sound she likes.

They discuss what happened earlier that day, surrounded by
medicine posters featuring Golden Retrievers.

She finishes the story about the Walker lady.
There is a long pause.
They talk about Japanese ice cream.
They talk about the problems of shooting the breeze and not learning anything.

"I'd love to teach you something, Scott. I want you to remember something
stark about life that will change you and make you less of an asshole."

She only used the word asshole for people she was attracted to.

"Well, we got five-and-a-half more hours. I'm sure you'll think of something,"
he replies and pulls two Pacifico beers out of the fridge from the dozen hiding
behind the plasma.

"Let's see. I got a whole bunch of strange stuff. I could tell you about how to
roll your last cigarette for a stranger in Prague, the importance of not listening
to sad music on the way to the airport, how to punch
someone in the throat with a lollipop stick or how to get rid of a hickey right
above your ass."

"Great. I get tons of those from vacuuming while drunk. Let's hear it."

"I could tell you now but you'd lose it. You should only tell people useful things
right before you split. People only remember the beginning and the end."
She flips the tone to electric piano on the control panel of her keyboard.
"This may seem off-topic. Do you like my name, Scott?"

"Why?"

"Every time I wash my hands, I see it in the mirror on my name tag and it just seems like a strike-less, meandering, forgettable name. Linda. Linnnduh. No guy screams out 'Oh Linda' during intercourse and doesn't secretly wish they were screaming out 'Oh Cassandra' or 'Oh Moesha.'

"Ya. But at least you're not a Stacy or Destiny. Those names force you into a life of stripping. It's true, you don't really look like a Linda. Maybe a Gaynell or a Pat."

"Scott, I'm serious. The last name is even more boring."

"What was your last name, Boxlightner?"

"Boxworthy. My father never sat us down and said, "Get in the game, kid, and fight. You're a Boxworthy. You are fuckin' worthy of many boxes and you must know this. In the days of yore, when other Lords were receiving gold, frankincense and myrrh... you'd get a big brown fuckin' box and this is what makes our heritage special."

"That's funny. Kinda."

"I know. Do you think I'm boring?"

"To be honest, I think your name is boring. But you're not boring. Especially a couple months ago when we got it on in the small room. Missionary on the metal table was a bit boring but other than that, I recall it as being pretty spur-of-the-moment and passionate. I still have bite marks. I tell people it's the Irish Setter."

There was a long pause which was acceptable 'cause there was music.

The scrambling of dog claws on cages and the hissing pace of cats became a tin melody with the sounds of the keyboard doing its soft digital thing.

Scott leaned across the counter towards her.
"Do you want to go pose the animals in the freezer? We could make it a contest."

"Not tonight."

"How about Dance Party USA?"

"What is that?"

"Come with me, Moesha."

They both coat the entire lobby floor with an inch-thick coat of water, then release all the dogs for a fifteen-minute romp while cranking 'Welcome To The Jungle' over the house stereo. They then put the frenzied dogs back in their cages and allow a fifteen-minute saunter for the kitties to the tune of 'Mr. Bojangles.' Cats love and always will love Sammy Davis Jr. for reasons that are self-evident.

Scott catches his breath and grabs Linda to set her on his lap. "I love seeing these sick animals romping like freshmen, but it is so against hospital policy. You know you could get fired, Linda?"

"Yes. Sure."

"I think it's worth it. Did you notice the dogs go crazy and slobber their brains out, crashing into walls like coked-out roller derby superstars, while the cats, during their shift, kind of walk about like Donald Trump
in a youth hostel with a look on their faces like, 'Seriously, this is bullshit."

"Sure."

Scott moves to kiss her while Linda stays as still as wax. Linda has locked her gaze at a spot on the floor. Scott touches her brown, unstyled hair.

"Hey. Heeey. What's the matter?"

Linda speaks low.

"I think animals have souls. I'm not gonna get too crazy about it. I can't prove that anything has a soul. It's just what I have chosen to believe after looking these living things in the eye day after day; you know, healing them, helping them die."

"Is there something you want to tell me?"

Linda starts breathing like the customer. Scott held her close to calm her down.
"It's O.K., babe. It's O.K."

46

He looks her in the eye and sees a woman daydreaming in a place he could never visit.

The feeling she had was much greater than the boredom she spoke of. It had choked the language from her.

She mumbles, "I wonder if when you name something, then it becomes real, or memorable. I wonder what a name does to a living thing."

Scott leans a mop across the white. "You sure do think of a lot of stuff when you ain't got shit to do. I brought you the good mop. Are you all right?"

"I just feel like talking. Like trying to figure this thing out."

"What thing? Are you sick? Do you need help with something? I can get just about anything pharmaceutical from Tijuana."

"No. I don't need you to solve. I just need you to listen. I can take care of things."

If Scott's brain were noisier there would be a ding sound.
"Are you depressed. Are you quitting? Are you pregnant?"

Linda bit her teeth. She did not cry.
"I was."

The air became twelve thousand pounds.
Scott was a logical man. He had a slow tongue and waited to speak until his chest stopped feeling funny. He wanted to say why didn't you tell me? He

wanted to say how dare you do this without me, but he knew he didn't know her well enough and probably would not love her.

"I read that animals abort spontaneously in stressful circumstances, without the grief that they show when a grown child dies."

Linda swabs at the tile.
"You don't have to say anything if you don't know what to say. I'm fine."

"Was it scary?"

"No. Yes. I remember writing on my hand I can hardly help dogs die, how can I help a human live?"

Scott stood his mop at attention in the bucket and took a deep breath.

"God, I feel dumb right now. I feel like...like I want to take that from you. I know I can't. I know I can't do that. I just feel like sorry is such a dumb thing to say. I'll just stop talking. Should I hold you for a second?"

"I don't need that."

"I want to."

They held each other that evening, standing among the hairballs and dirty mop water of the animal shelters lobby floor. A scene you will never see when you go to bring in your poodle for a vaccination. A scene that plays out differently in different places on different days throughout the world. People with different names wondering about the same things, while creatures with no names run around the wilderness, the air and the sea, loathing capture, needing no legacy or tombstone.

Here two forgettable, broken creatures stood, holding each other until the dogs, cats, birds and snakes laid down in their cages, held still for a moment, their names locked around their necks, watching a moment unfold, unable to comprehend it...but remembering all of it.

SGT. PEDERSON WOULD LIKE A WORD WITH YOU

Put your mouth in the lean and rest, sucker and bite down on this sweet pill of misery and wonder known as my fartbox of a life. Lock your beady little eyeballs on these pages and suckle on the empty tits of losing, you ungrateful Toilets. Read this closely and learn, buttwads. Your days of being ate up are over. You can win.

You don't have to live a life of total black darkness. You stay alert, you stay alive, soldier. Let me tell you somethin.' I was born for two things. Defense of my country, loving my family and for pleasuring ladies. Not so successful with the latter. I'm a big enough man to admit that. I'm starting to think women don't understand Sgt. Pederson. I was known as The Midwestern Love Tank. No one actually called me that cause it was too long to say, but it's understood. You can learn from my mistakes. I have been born again. Learn from me privates, learn from me. A happy soldier is a worse warrior, but a smarter citizen. Put your shoe to your ear and Get Smart or die like a dummy.

I'm starting to think Sgt. Pederson shouldn't write or talk in the third person, but he can't help it. Third person helps reveal some of Sgt. Pederson's insecurities.

He knows when the insecurity started. His English teacher told him to 'write it all down' to help relieve the pain. O.K. This is me writing it down. This is where the trouble began.

My last girlfriend came over for a little Valentine's Day hob-nobbing. It was February 14th. I really liked her, so what?

To be honest, I was sprung. She had a whole kit. Candles and smelly candles, flowers, crèmes and all kinds of useless stuff prefixed with either the word butter or cocoa or tea tree. None of it edible. Isn't that dumb? I was surprised to be actually relaxed with the whole frou-frou thing. I tried to get into it. Just kidding.

Sgt. Pederson thinks overt home decor and perfumed bathing supplies is a sign of weakness. BUT! I went with the flow. I shaved. I trimmed my back pubes and showered with a rag. I even wrote a poem. You damn skippy I ain't showing it to you though, turd.

So she broke out a bottle of somethin' and looked at me lovely and seductively.
I thought we were on the same wavelength. I tried to do the same.
We were both orderly and liked to feel good. Sex feels good.
We should like sex...a lot. It's just a back massage for your interior so what's the big deal.
Turns out most female contraptions don't always work that way.
This is where our plot goes all squirrelly.

Her hips rocked toward me like she was hot stuff.
She was chubby and she was my lady.
"Honey," she said, "loooook what I got."

"What is that? Shampoo?"

"Nooooo dear. It's something else. It's...lotion. Do you know what that means?"

"Um. You damn right I do, baby."

"You do, you big bear? Tell me."

Her voice was sliding into a comfortable purr.
This kitty needed Daddy's catnip. I didn't know she was naughty. It's always the nice girls. Pastors' daughters, union people, people with library cards.

"You want me to say it out loud?" I said.

"Yesssss." I could smell the slut venom flitting in her jeans. "Ssssay it."

"O.K ...you want me to give you a...backstage pass?"

"What?" I could tell she was playing frisky and kind of wanted me to say it again.

"You dirty bird. You want ol' Brer Rabbit to thump on your briar patch, dontcha, dontcha?"

"Oh my God."

Her jaw fell open like an audience at a catastrophe. I thought she was wowed by my knowledge, I thought to myself "I don't know much about this role playing shit but I will continue in this sneaky little poopie chute love game." Not giving away too much. I said,

"Baby, I been dreaming of dipping your doughnut hole since day one. You are a kinky broad. This is why I think I'm falling in love with you." She looked like she was gonna cry.

"You-are-the-grossest pervert in all of Fort Sill. When I told you I was anal, I meant I was organized." Tears.

"Baby. You know that's a lie. Private Addington is way grosser than me. He dressed like C-3PO and did the cottage cheese thing to a crippled Weimariner. I ain't into that creative shit. You know me. Baby?"

"You...I can't...Ya know, you think you really know someone. Michael. Just leave and never talk to me again except to get your things. Don't call me for at least two weeks. I don't want to see your face."

Margaret shoved me into the doorway. I didn't shove back 'cause my buddy went to jail for breaking a plate when his wife and him got in an argument. Margaret and I had been together for ten months. I couldn't touch her. It was instinct to snap a neck when someone touched me, but I fought it. She was my first real girlfriend so she deserved better. It doesn't seem like a long time to date but it was long enough for me to cry in front of her when we watched Full Metal Jacket.

"Wait. I wrote you a poem." I said this when she was already in the driveway.

I wish you could hear little sound effects in my journal. I guess I could write a little "WHAM" or a "KASLAMM" 'cause you know, I felt that sound in my chest.

God, I talk too much. I think I know what people mean when they say 'be honest.' I try and I am always wrong when I talk too much.
No one really wants honesty or I'd tell you how ugly you are,
but just on the outside, or you're fat but I'd still do you.
I'm trying to say that we aren't perfect and imperfection is sexy but everything comes out stupid. I said too much.

Man, what a horrible night that was. I was so ready to be loving, caring, and to work her trench into an overweight, sweaty Valentine's mess. I'm talking total romance. "The best line of the poem can be considered foreplay," my teacher once said. I'll sneak you one of the lines from Margaret's poem wrote "Your bathing suit area is a clock, Margaret. For it takes a licking and keeps on ticking." Isn't that nice? I'm talkin' about love and beach stuff. Look at me.

I treat love really well. How love treats you is a whole different bag of soup. Love is something that will take you by the throat if you don't take it by the throat first and hang on until it croaks in your clutches. If it bleeds all over you, then the blood gets on your fingers and you lose your grip on your chokehold and then you gotta stab it in the face.

Maybe that's a bad analogy.

How about this: Love is like humping. If you can avoid it all your life, you'll be all right, but once you dare to have a morsel of its slippery delight, then you always want it and you're a walking time bomb without it.

I can't tell you to avoid it though. You have been designed to find the grapes of love and suckle them. That's God, ya'all. Just don't fall as hard as I did. Focus on your craft, your work. Focusing on love makes you a looney bird.

Ladies, this goes for you too. Get promoted. Work your ass off and you'll get too busy to be heartbroken. I was working on getting my E-6 when all this went down. I got a letter from CentCom that said "Attention Sergeant Pederson; In order to be considered for Staff Sergeant promotion you must successfully complete at least five units of college credit in order to be fit to blah blah blah."

Great. Civilians. School again. The only class that didn't conflict with Pathfinder school was creative writing.

I was very disinterested, to say the least, until Private Farkas told me about a writer named Ernest Something who blew his brains out with a shotgun. That touched me and saddened me. I didn't even know he was dead. I had seen all the movies including "Ernest Goes To Camp" and the vacation one and thought I'd go as a sort of homage.

The syllabus said Creative Writing 101 and I was like, 'shit, that sounds a little advanced. I am probably like a Creative Writing 5 or 6 kind of guy.'

The last creative thing I did was to disassemble and clean an M-16-A1, air-cooled, gas-operated, semi-and fully automatic weapon blindfolded while singing the theme to the hit T.V. show 'Family Ties.' Oh, and I can eat all the cream out of a red coconut Zinger, but that's it.

The first day I felt very out of place. You see, there are a few reasons why a guy joins the Army:

1. You're from a place like Gary, Indiana. 'Nuff said.
2. You're stupid and couldn't get a scholarship.
3. You had asshole parents and the Army gives you a proud new family to belong to.
4. You like to shower naked with grown men of many nations.

I think I'm number 2 or 4. I'm kidding. Most kids in this class look like they could star in their own reality show called 67-Sided Dice Unbound, My Life With Dungeons and Dragons.

There was this one Asian girl in class that was giving me the kind of look that you can't see, but you can feel. She was kinda fat like Margaret and I liked it.

We had to write something the first day. I...wrote about Margaret and how much I missed her. It sucked.

That Asian girl wrote about revenge and some weirdo stuff. It was beautiful. Her name was Julie Gish or Dish or Chin or Nguyen. She wrote in her piece,

"I have abandoned the factory of men.
I have re-charged the seamstresses' nightmares.
Crawling up the lighthouse.
I have the sailors all hanging
by gold threads with sand in their pockets.
A desperate insomniac whispers your skin
into a bed and sleeps like a tick.
Your blood is locked in its mouth.
Sunlight is always hitting me so I must speak to hit back.
This is me, darling.
I take what I want."

My first thought was "Holy shit."
My second thought was "I'd do her."
My third thought was maybe she could tutor me,
to write a poem that would help me win Margaret back.

I'll skip all the boring stuff. She said she'd help me. Julie asked what I did for
a living. I said I kill things when the government asks me to. I lead the guard
duty for the motor pool; I clean artillery muzzles for night ops and heavy
drops and run operations on the firing range for the Mark 19. How about you?

She said, "I party."

She smiled slow and wide like she had won. She trained me for about 4 weeks.
Taught me about details, craft and control. We met every
day and she gave me books by Faulkner, Vonnegut and Miller. I read the back
of every single one and I learned a lot.

I tried to notice things. Tiny things.
Eyelashes. A lady's strut. A dog's snot. The face of a kid denied ice cream
before he starts bawling. She showed me how to hold it all. She "delivered me
into the details," she said.

She was smart and sad as fuck. She knew exactly how to say things. There was
the hurt and she was in it and showing all of it.

"Seems like you're hiding something, Jules. Or running from something."

"Some women aren't running from anything. Some wait for things to run to
them and they live in an advent calendar, counting the days until the things
they need or love walk away or get their guts ran over by a bus. Women like me
settle in their sadness like a cat pawing a pillow. It's OK."

She has had a lot of stuff go astray for such a young girl.
She wouldn't want me to tell you because it's private. All this noticing, it was the
first time I felt like I wasn't losing. I hope you're still learning from this.

"Look out behind you, dead meat!" was the name of my first poem. It went
like this.

Look out behind you, dead meat!
That's what you say when you stab a rack of tires in Basic.
I see love in many ways.

Mostly as a rack of radials
you just keep jabbing and stabbing
until it dies in the midst of this obstacle course.
I don't know if it was ever alive before,
but it sure feels good getting a chance to bash the crap out of it.
I'm not sure what I'm saying here.

The teacher the next day made me read my newest poem in front of the whole
class. I was shaking like a box of maracas. I had trouble breathing.
Julie rubbed my shoulders and slapped me on the ass like she was Vince Lombardi.
She worked withme a lot on it and I thanked her for being hot and not letting
me sleep with her and for all the advice. I made my way to the front.

"This new is... is called 'I Fall For You in Autumn.'

Margaret, your skin is shinier than a platoon of new jump boots.
Your laugh is a grenade in the chest
of a child that thought he was indestructible.
Your hair is hiding all the camouflaged wonder of your mind.
I want to curl the brown of it around these gunpowder fingers.
If found by the Ranger who needs you,
He will dream tonight of the weapons in your hips.
I'm the love tank, Margaret. My treads have been blown.

Pay attention, young soldiers. Whether I got Margaret back or not doesn't
matter. This feeling, or feeling, is the act of not losing. This I give back to you,
the same way Margaret gave herself back to me. This is one blind idiot telling
the world "I see you sucker." You can stand up and say "I am not a victim or
a passenger. I am the one fuckin' the duck around here.
You just stand back and watch the feathers fly." Carry on.

HOW TO LEAVE THE OZARKS

March 3.

If you have found this journal, I hope you are reading it slowly.

I am in Arkansas still. I am still in Arkansas.

The wind is hurling itself against the meadows;
It comes to the hotel windows
as a low song from a record played too fast.

To me, the wind is a Victrola.
It is born to howl these ballads.

I am here in this hotel to figure out how to be.
I wonder if this feeling has ever crossed you.

When the big 'life' question is asked—
it's always Why, but I want to know How,
How to keep goin',
when you just don't feel like goin' anymore.
When are you done?

The engine is underwater.

This storm grinds its wet stuff against the exterior walls of this room
and the raindrops cruise tiny applause across my balcony window.

I think of all the lovemaking I've never done.

I've been staying here on the eleventh floor of the Radisson
in Fayetteville, Arkansas
for the last 2 weeks.

There is the thick black Gideon book on the nightstand that I can't start.
There is a story here that needs a finish.

I'd like to choose my ending.
You could call it 'A rebellion on God's surprises.'

I just have to pick the ending.
Where do we find a good ending?
In the lost index of a love novel?
In the catalogued files of our misery?
In the confidential losses of the living?
In the Radisson?

I can't stay here. I am almost out of money.

I need a beer and 50,000 dollars.

Every night before I sleep
I remember the question slumber party kids would ask
'Is it better to drown slow or burn alive fast?'
The question for me has always been
'Do I want people to remember the smoke
or the fire?'

I heard of a Navy veteran who outmaneuvered Kamikaze pilots in WW2
and then died at age 78 from a West Nile virus mosquito bite.
I feel like if I want to die in a rebellion or by skydiving into the roof of the
Oval Office without a chute.
What I'll really get is a slip on a soapy loofah,
concussion in the bathtub.

If you want die to die valiantly,
 rescuing someone from a building or saving a baby from a car crash,
you'll probably just get testicular cancer.

Some stories end well. Some just slam on the brakes.

I paid cash to the friendlies at the front desk.
I wanted no visitors.
I am room 1101.
The window is locked.
I haven't opened it. Weird having a window burglar lock eleven stories up.
I thought all the giants died in the '60s.

Someone had been smoking in my room.
It smells like my Father and I remember bronchitis.

The art isn't nailed down which means this is classy for me.
The stale starch in the bedspread. The unoffensive everything.
This feels like a good place to have surgery or an affair.

I use the whole shotgun-shell-sized hotel conditioner bottle every night.
All
over my body.
I feel rich and my arm hairs get soft as...I dunno.
Not a baby's ass. That's a fallacy.
Babies don't actually have softer asses.
People just don't touch naked babies as hard.
What am I talking about? I've been alone for too long.

I'd really like to go home but I know they're waiting for me.
Sneaky little beavers.
There's no way I am gonna spend another year, for them,
with the retards at that idiot clinic.
Unless they catch me.
I can't let them catch me.

I remember, six months in, some in the group at the clinic who were also sent
by loved ones actually started believing they were sick with an affliction cause
they had at least ...seven drinks a work week. I'm not kidding.

Europeans would wet their pants if they heard that. Every day, as the counselor
talked us through his coma monologue, I would yell out something in the middle.
Not because I really hate the guy, I just hate what this whole thing is really
about...and I was feelin' horny.

I think his name was Michel. A soft, faraway name. He spoke like he was from
a commune in Arizona.

"...No, I don't think it takes vision to see who we really, really really are, but
that amazing moment is hiding where we release and say I am worth..."

"TITS!" I'd bolt out.

"...er, uh I'm sorry, question? No? O.K. um...and the real thing is to watch
honest-to-goodness joy flow abundantly, truly abundantly..."

"PEEEEENIIIIIS."

"Who? Who? No question? O.K. Today is a new day and it's really about just really letting the self encourage you. If we could just really look inside ourselves, not at what you see, but to look inside ourselves and see what you are…"

Then something inside me really started to hate this poor guy. I lost it.

"Look inside ourselves? I suggest a personal X-ray for yourself, you heartless, illegitimate, crystal-vortex-riding hippie."
Blood rushed to my tongue.
I had just seen One Flew Over the Cuckoo's Nest before all this went down.

"I'm tired of you telling me to look inside myself 'cause you can't come up with any real advice. Is everything a disease? When are we allowed to die? Even if it's slow. Gimme the damn choice at least. That's freedom, assholes.
I've seen alcoholics and this ain't it. Thanks for the fancy commitment coins and the mantras. I'll make my own. You should be out there on the street helping the homeless get on the wagon. They're out there waiting for you, freezin' and drinking just so they can fall asleep.
Why don't you wrap up your little pity party so we don't have to keep sitting here feeling guilty while you chase the air.

You're a Sasquatch hunter.
You're a Loch Ness handjob.
You conjure fear harder than the 11'o clock news, begging us to confess our normalities so you can make an easy paycheck while your nipples turn to rockets every time we cry, symptoms you invented, you filthy walking pile of organic, touchy-feely overanalyzed ass. I wipe you. I wipe you away."

Wham. I got another six months in the treatment center under high security.
That diatribe wanted out more than I did.
Let's call it, Senioritis. There's a disease. I'll call Pfizer.

I was treated like a psycho after that and I probably deserved it.
I put a Bible verse on my wall to show I was making progress.

Proverbs 31:6. "Give strong drink unto him that is ready to perish, and wine unto those that be of heavy hearts. Let him drink and forget his poverty and remember his misery no more."
Thought it was funny.

All the guys really wanted me after that which is nice, except for the fact that
all the guys in there were already broken.
They weren't alive.
I wasn't attracted.

My parents had begun to sell my personal things to pay for treatment.
I don't know what to tell you...it's just the worst feeling.

You ever been lost in a department store as a kid?
Hiding in the clothes racks,
longing for your mother to slide her hands in
and take you from the polyester slacks?
That'd be nice. I dreamt of that last night. As if the world was a whole
bunch of pants
and I was just waiting for someone to find me and take me home.

March 4.
The wind is picking up wonderfully outside.
Sounds like an African elephant shot in the face
gaining anger and release.

The Ozarks are getting darker than a tar pit of widows.

Someone slid a note under my door.
I thought it was an eviction notice. I didn't pay for last night.
It said "Tornado warning in full effect.
If you hear the smoke detector siren, take refuge in the stairwell. Thanks.
The management."
I stepped to the beige disc on the ceiling and pulled it apart.
Someone had removed the battery so they could smoke.
Good for them.

What I really want is a beer.

I don't need it, I just want it...wish I could afford a case.
My parents think I need it.
They don't know what I need.

March 5.
I watched T.V. all day,
roaming the morning halls
for leftovers on plates and in the bottles of champagne.
All of this, 'cause of them.
They were so obsessed with showing me how to live right
they put my spirit in a chalk outline.

I stare out the soft focus of smeared balcony glass
through the storm.
I think of all those people,
all those problems.

God is not trying to fix the unfixable.
so what the hell are we doin'?
He set this mother in motion and let it go.
He is not trying to heal those that don't want to be healed.
Stuff breaks down for a reason.
Sometimes you should just let it be.
I just want to feel good.
I just want to feel incredible.
I just want a great ending.

March 6.
It sounded just the way I spell it now,
KEEERRRRASSSSHHH!

Holy shit! Glass everywhere.
The wind is pinning the blankets into wallpaper.
A cursing kind of wind peaking at the center of the room.
Hair straps across my face.
Something has just burst through the glass of my balcony window.
It is rolled like a huge cigarette, covered in a curtain.
I ran into the bathroom and just slammed the door.

Fear is born inside me. I can't do anything but write this down.

Quiet. Calm down. Exhale. Lord.
I'm going to go out there and see what it is..........................

I thought the twister must have launched a log
through my window.

I opened the bathroom door,
peeked out.
I saw the lamp became toast.
The carpet's got wet.
The wind is high but dying down.
The phone is off the hook and beeping. It's cold.

Something was rolled in the fabric of the curtain.

I moved towards the stuff on the wall. It looked like paint. It looked like blood.

It was blood.

A moan came out of the curtain on the floor. It was a man. I couldn't tell his age.
There was blood painting his neck and face.
His leg are mangled.
I unwrapped him from the cloth and sat him up on my bed.

I could envision his body lifting from some tractor and feeling the moment
when gravity vanishes.
Trailer pieces, trees and cars whirling about him. Narrowly missing his skull.
A balcony window zooming towards his face.

He is hurting, out there, wheezing.
I wiped the red and the mud from his eyes.
His retinas were wide with adrenaline.
He is dressed in farming overalls, maybe in his 20s. He's still out there.

I wanted to ask him what happened, but I couldn't stop staring at his eyes.
My heartbeat is climbing right now as I write this.
I've never seen his countenance on a person before.

I felt as if I was staring the universe, all the ages, right in the face.
I couldn't stop for a bit. I couldn't believe he was still alive.
His eyes were blasting electricity into my spine.
His spirit formed a power plant around me.

He held my hand.
There was. He squeezed my hand and said, "help me."

I began bleeding a little from the shards, into his blood and felt no pain.
He gripped my hand tightly and his lips were trembling like California.

He spoke with a great pain in his voice, "I can't...uh, move.
We...are in...the eye of...storm...for now,
it will come back.
I don't want it to grab me again. My back.
Am I gonna die? I don't want to die. I don't want to."

His teeth showed through the rust on his face.
He was without blinking.
I helped him to the safety of the bathtub and gave him towels for bandages.

He is next to me.

I told him he was going to be fine. That he was going to live and will feel
better tomorrow. I told him to relax.

I am going to prop the hall door open so they can find him.
I am going to move to the window in a moment.

I am not depressed. I am not drunk. I am tired of the gravity.
I am choosing my ending, hard on the brakes.

I stand on the edge of the balcony.
The wind begins to swell around me.
I listen to its song. I've sung that song.

I am done.

YOU, MY DEAR,
ARE A VERY SPECIAL STARFISH

Text of the first graduation speech delivered by famed dramatist Lydia Handlestock on the moon, June 18, 2028

It is immaculately quiet in here. Do you know why? Because you're here...and you're here because you're rich...and because you're rich you're well mannered and because you're well-mannered...you don't test the rules. And because you don't test the rules, your performances last night were the equivalent of a puppet show done by dead monkey cadavers...and yes, it was redundant on purpose. It was prison sex with Neil Simon and a looped yawn for an orgasm. You were cartoons drawn by cartoons. You're a cheerleader with a boner and no quarterbacks to pile at the party. You are CONFUSED BY PASSION. You can't control or summon the force of ridiculous triggers inside you like my students on Earth do.

But so help me, as God keeps holding this blue gun to my head. By the end of this address, you will stop being a bunch of interstellar doorknobs. You will know passion. You must know passion. LYDIA HANDLESTOCK PASSION.

And now I will sing. Why? Because I do whatever I want. Aaaaaaa.

Listen, I don't know what they're teaching you pinko, snot-nosed goobers up here on Mars but I sure as hell hope you know who George S. Patton is.

General George S. Patton was King Shit. He had the curse of mandatory victory inside him. Comparatively, he was the greatest warrior of the twentieth century. He said something...to the effect of...

"Men, I know some of you are concerned about whether you'll chicken out under fire when you're in those trenches. Well, I guarantee you, when you put your hand into a pile of goo that moments before was your best friend's face, well...you'll know what to do."

It is gory, heartfelt, weirdo brilliance. You didn't let us, the audience place our hands into your goo last night. Don't hide it under a bushel, give us the goo!

Now, listen, in truth, Patton was a fumbling dolt of a man. Comparatively, take any passionate warrior of the last 300 years and place them next to Lydia Handlestock and I will overshadow them like the moon to sun. I put the Lips in Eclipse, the Cat and the Skills in the Catskills, now suck it.

Listen, I'm not trying to berate you or lift myself up up up. You see, if I disturb you.. you will feel something and that is the first step to recovering your...oh, how do they put it in Indonesia...your nuts. I don't know what happened to you kids up here on Mars but it seems like when you're surround yourselves with nothing possibility vanishes. Passion turns vanilla.

You know, I came here with great enthusiasm. I used to think that space was our last ocean, a place we dumped wishes not people. Not our future. I know that each and every one of your parents is secretly aroused by the idea of educating your child on Mars for one million dollars...but it's vain.. so unnecessary.
I mean, have you seen the smooth skin of Spain. Felt the heaviness of Ravensburg or seen the gorgeous transvestites of San Francisco.

I'm telling you, you don't need to travel to gain experience. What you need are bad experiences because right now all of you are a bunch of sexless, drug-less, storyless derivatives of your parents...blaaaah. More singing. Aaaaa.

Maybe I cam down a bit hard on you. Don't get me wrong, your performances last night were...atrocious. However, I realize now, that maybe you aren't the source.

I have a gift to give you and if you can all stop being nerdy pricks for two seconds I will.

You see, I stand here with a heart full of failures where valves used to be. Veins I used like cables to pull myself from one shit hole to the next. Thighs like steering wheels from having my legs at ten and two too many times. My life became like space...black, black, black...with little specks of white.

Now, who here knows why I'm saying this you in the middle of what should have been a very normal commencement address.

That's right, because I did have one prepared…This address was going to be…blah blah reach for the stars…blah blah go for your dreams…a lotta outer space puns and alien fondling jokes. Starfish have no brains, don't be a starfish, be a star, I had a coupla great Battlestar Galacta zingers too…oh well.

What's honest is more important. Honest passion is a good performance.

Lesson one in this passion play.

Enjoy getting ripped a new donut hole.
Let's start with last night's gig. The Orion Theatre. 1900 hours.
Curtain. You played a college kid who hot boxes his space pod hookah who wants to be a hit man but deep down inside he's a good guy. You made me wish I was stoned…as in BEAT TO THE DEATH WITH VERY SMALL ROCKS.

His best friend here is gay with AIDS and cancer.
What a winning combination! Throw in retarded and you've got the trifecta.
You win the Oscar but not my attention.

Listen, make fun of what you hold dear. Don't respect anything too much. Let fear guide you. You write your brains out, you perform your brains, you fuck your brains out on the carcasses of critics…and you let people with hang ups deal with their own mazes inside of themselves. You say to them, "Fuck you, I'm right, you're empty now you owe mama head you walking complex."

Now.

Lesson two.

Go hungry for your art, but don't starve.

I have starved. I have so starved in the middle of my own storms.

Huh? Let me explain to you the song of the starving Sea Lion.

On Earth there is a cold region known as Antarctica. Sea Lions quietly roam under vast glowing miles of blue ice. Swimming in the quiet and most heavenly arena of underwater glaciers while storms riot above them. They need air holes in the ice to breathe and the sea lions keep the holes open by munching them with their teeth but.. they need their teeth to hunt.
So they can either starve to death or suffocate to death. Sea lions die young... the older ones are weak and skinny. Still breathing. Still wishing they had teeth... but there's just too many storms pushing too much ice. Do you know why I'm saying this?

(to an offstage character)

No. No. I don't want the pills today.

Why? Because I'm talking to the kids.

What do you mean, what kids? The kids right here. You can't see them?

Well, they can't see you...Just let me finish...Don't touch me! Don't you touch me! I NEED TO AAAAGH. FINE, I WILL TAKE YOUR DAMN PILLS!

It's just...I was feeling something...
just promise me you'll finish telling them what I was talking about...it goes like this...

black, black, black, with little specks of white...got it?
black, black, black...with little specks...
of white.
x

THE ROYAL DOGS OF TEXAS

Hummingbirds. Always seems like there are hummingbirds everywhere in
the South, stealin' juice cause their instinct can do no other. A hunter cracks
peanuts in his deer stand. Not a serious hunter. Not the kind that needs to eat.
The other kind. The kind who shoots stuff as a hobby. A pick-up truck backfires.
A mosquito dies between the applause of a hand and a neck.
The trees do their slave dance. The sun is out for blood. Ice cubes rattle in a
tea glass.
A screen door yawns like a baby waking up.

Other than that, stillness.

Few places are quieter than Alto, Texas. I'm not sure if I should tell you why.

This part of the land is teeming with quiet desolation. Desperate places make
everyone shut-up.

It is strange. No one talks about what happened to John T. Royal. No one talks.
The only one I commiserate with is Merle.
I always say the same joke to him when I see him.
"How's the day Merle? You look a little Haggard."
When he looks up, it looks like he's about to spit.
"The day is what it is, Tom."

The years have not been good to Merle. We got close cause he's old and gets
the stomach flu and I'd come over and give him some 7-up and place a wet
towel on his butthole. He says it's the best feelin' and we joke about it. He's
from Austin so he's weird. I don't know what he's doin' here. He don't
know what he's doin here. He is the only man I know without photographs.
You figure a man in his late 70's would have some pictures, and if he didn't
have pictures, he must be holdin' a whole world o'hurt that he never wanted to
see again.

He kinda holds his hurt in his shoulders and I try and drag conversation out
of him.

"You never ever told me 'bout what you used to do." I spun the cubes in my
tea. His tea always had tea leave chunks in it and the flavor was a bit bitter.
It was always cold and cold beats flavor any day in the South.

"Lots of stuff I suppose." Merle wiped the drool from his pillow as he laid face down next to the wood paneling on a cheap cot. "It musta been 30 some odd years ago."

"Well, like what. Shoot me straight."

"Government work, you know. Not Spy stuff or anything. Straight."
Merle closed his eyes.

"You plant trees with nerds? Spill it. You one of those Rambo types that don't like talkin' about it?"

He rolled over onto his back and sat up. "No. I'll tell you. I don't know why I feel like tellin' you. Maybe cause it's been bottled up too long. I worked for the Secret Service when I was older than you. I had been applying for 6 years and when I made it to the fourth level and passed, I moved from Alto to D.C."

"You guarded the president?" I wasn't gonna believe him but thought I'd listen and might have a good chuckle, depending on how grand the lies were.

"No. His wife. She was a great lady. Wife of the 37th president. Her name was Pat, Pat Nixon. Born in Nevada. Named after St. Patrick. Ma died at 13, Pa, passed at 18.
Amazing woman. She got a job as a janitor and made her own way. Tough lady. A real lady. She shook everyone's hand. Even lepers in Panama. She got real close to people till there was no one left to meet."

The details pulled me deeper into the truth. I can smell a bullshitter. This was the real deal. Merle looked nervous, like he was about to propose.

"I shot someone. I made a mistake."

"Uh huh." I tried to make it seem like that's what secret service agents do. I tried to pass him the honey roasted peanuts, but his mind had gone elsewhere and ignored me.
His breath began to quiver. He reached over and turned on the lamp.

"I shot someone. I shot Bill Baumdart in the service of the first lady, Pat Nixon. I severed a portion of his spinal cord with the bullet and he couldn't walk for the rest of his life. News said he was a track and field coach. He's dead now from old age. Every day that passes, the more I get near the end, I get more scared.

I'm scared to meet him up there, Tom. I don't wanna die."

"Jesus."

"I made a mistake, Tom. I think about it every long day. He leaped a barrier to get an autograph as she was getting in the limousine. You can't do that. The barrier was blue and said 'police' on it. I watched him running towards the car and readied my pistol. I hadn't slept in about 2 days, Tom. The Gov works ya like a dog when they're short-handed. I loved working with Pat. I woulda died for her. They let me go at her request but didn't press charges. They told me to vanish. I never saw Pat again. That's all I wanted. I came back. I been here, sittin' around, Tom."

Merle kept saying my name at the end of his sentences and it kept sounding like the deepest, hardest, scarlet of grief. He turned out the light, realizing he had turned it on for no reason.

I stood up and didn't really know what to say. "I'm gonna go grab some booze. You need to cheer up and let shit like that go. It's their fault for overworkin' ya, right?"

"Hm. Booze ain't gonna make me smile, Tom. You know that. I ain't that type. But damn right I'll take some."

"Have you ever smiled, Merle?"

I could see his eyes scrolling backwards through that dark memory box. "Yes. When I was a boy. When I was a little boy."

"And you don't have any pictures of it."

"No. I don't. Uh, I know of one in existence but I don't have it. I don't need to have it."

I had never seen Merle talk this much sober. There were little white cobwebs of saliva forming at the corners of his mouth. I grabbed a dishrag and wiped 'em clean.

"You gonna tell me where that picture is, Captain. No one's gonna believe you ever smiled without a photograph to prove it."

"I think I gave it to John Royal, years ago for buying me a baseball bat when I was a kid. He's gone too. He told me to hit as many home runs and break as many windows as possible. 12. I dunno if he kept the portrait. That place is a shithole flophouse now. John Royal was a good man."

"Well you know what, I'm fixin' to get us some Coors Light and I'm gonna take a peek and I'll be right back."

Merle stood. Merle rarely stood and he spoke with a gravelly fear in his throat.

"Do not go on that property. Forget it, Tom. Please."

"No one's gonna...Oh. Come on, Merle. You don't believe that stuff about the devil haunting Royal's joint do you? That's crap the Baptists made up to keep people from desecrating his property."

"It ain't the devil, Tom. I been there and it feels...it feels heavy. I'm sure the place has been ransacked by kids anyway. I'm sorry. It just ain't worth it, it just ain't worth your time, that's all."

" O.K. relax. I'll be back in a spell. You want PBR, tall boys or Coors Light?"

"Anything's fine. Coors Light. Tom. I'm serious."

"I know. I know."

Driving down FM180, he had to know that I couldn't help myself. It would be like gold to see Ol' Merle smilin' like a shiny nickel, even if it was in black and white.

I needed to make him remember. If the place was trashed, it would make me want to go inside even more, especially if folks were still saying it was haunted.

I think remembering is good. I once thought I was in love again because a song was playing on the radio by Johnny Cash. 'The first time, ever I saw your face..." It made me remember exactly how I felt holding my wife to be in the storm outside the A+W rootbeer. We got rain inside of our root beer floats and drank 'em anyway. That divorce cleared years ago.

How does one go from being a real daisy to a screeching, ball twisting, hog of a bitch? It is mind blowin' isn't it? The answer is, you stop remembering your root beer and you only see the dirty laundry.

I had to make him remember something good before he passed away.
I felt like he had months now.
I thought it'd do him some good to remember his youth.
You look at bastards on T.V. The lawyers and the superstars. You forget they used to be kids. You stare down at the person you're fuckin' and you forget they used to not know how to talk. You gotta remember.

John T. Royal's grounds are a bit creepy. Bums used to live here. He left his home to nobody. I guess he didn't have much time to write one on account of the feds blowin' his brains out. The state didn't want it cause there was too much drama surrounding it after his murder.

The weeds are tall and sweeping. It looks like a plantation after the civil war. Smells like sage.
Some say where I stand is hallowed ground.

There are dogs in this soil.

I don't mean bad men. I mean dogs. Hundreds of loyal dogs.
Some were killed by rifle...and some were buried alive. Let me tell you about it.

John T. Royal was a loner, claimed to have a mirror factory. No one knew what kind of equipment that needed, so no one questioned the strange machines on his property. The feds spotted it and figured it to be a moonshine business. This was a dry town in the driest of times. The story goes that they sent two agents in to talk with John.

John Royal was Irish so they shoulda expected a bit of a fireball. What they didn't expect was a valley of dogs. Hundreds of them. Eatin' each others bones. Wallowing in the heaven of the wilderness, waiting to protect their master, at any cost.

Those two agents never returned to headquarters. Rumor had it that John sicked the dogs on 'em to eat em to death. One week later, the Feds just about called out the whole Texas National Guard, and they wanted that boy's head.

One of the soldiers misfired a shot at a dog trying to gnaw through the fence and John Royal came out with guns blazing, firing with vengeance and people around here knew his aim was true.

He had sawed off shotguns strapped to his legs and revolvers holstered on the inside of his pants. Papers said he was in a rage. The dogs were protecting him, piling their bodies in front of him like bunkers. They said with every dog that went down, John would whistle, drop to the ground and reload behind the carcass of a Rottweiler or Great Dane. When he finally went down, which reports say did take awhile, John T. Royal let out some sort of chirp and the other hundred or so dogs halted and sat at attention. Quiet and no longer growling.

The toll was 22
guardsmen down, 113 dogs and one John T. Royal. The guard, moved in and on command massacred those dogs. Every one of them. They were smart dogs and they were plain murdered. The ones that were still breathing, they buried them too and tossed John's body in the mass grave with them. It was a mess and this was the most effective way they could devise to clean it up. The sad part is they never found the bodies of those two agents, who some say were waxed by The Italians in Houston.

I enter the house and it does feel heavy. It doesn't amaze me that there is graffiti everywhere or mud, but there are little broken pieces of mirrors all over the floor. There is a wind whipping through this house that wasn't outside. It smells like piss. I have no idea where to look. I'm sure there's rats in every drawer.

I feel this amazing sensation wash over me and I close my eyes. I begin walking. I am now in the basement. I am being led. My hand lifts and touches a handle on a cupboard. I open my eyes.

There is no need for me to tell you what I saw because you wouldn't believe me. But I know this for sure. He was making mirrors and he was making moonshine and I will never return to that house.

An hour later I pulled up to Merle's raggedy trailer.
I handed him a can of mildly warm beer and behind the can was the picture.
He touched it and began weeping.

"Oh my God. You found it. Lord, I was a runt. I remember those shoes and
how they always smelled terrible. My mother made those shorts out
of..."

We both kinda smiled. Merle's smile still looked he was about to spit. It's good
to notice. It's good to remember. I'll start with the morning.

The sun.
A screen door.
Ice cubes.
Trees.
A mosquito.
A pick-up truck.
Hummingbirds.
A field where cats are afraid to cross.

THE WEAPONS FORMED AGAINST ME
DID PROSPER

There is a bar in in town where people want to talk to me
about more than just the weather.

Someone always buys for me, which is a perk.
After the first shot I talk about the town and progress.

The second shot I break discourse on politics and the need for making the
discourse on good blowjobs less taboo.

The third shot I kinda just sit there, connivin' about how to get back into a rig
and of course about how much I miss blowjobs.

The fourth shot I drift into the premise of who I would kill for 50 dollars,
which often leads to the Easter Bunny and Phil Collins takin' the top slots.

And the fifth shot gets me talkin' about the nature of black angels.
It's not that it's all I wanna talk about.
It's all people wanna hear. I might be the only one who knows.

I'll tell you.

It was a strong beast. It was a supernatural experience real enough to send
an agnostic knee first to choir practice.

Whether you believe it or not, I know what I saw.

A lot of folks ask me what the difference is between angels and demons.
Well, not much except one is ugly as dog shit and shoots fire out his ass and
pisses hot lava.

I seen both. But I actually couldn't tell the difference. Demons usually got
long chins and hefty limps from fallin' to earth. Angels don't wear white or
showboat their wings. But they do carry electricity and whisper a lot. Does
this sound crazy? Shit's biblical.

First off I must have you know that I am not insane and I am not a certifiable drunk.
I do drink a Gentleman jack Granddad on special days only. It ain't my
fault that the good Lord made every day feel special to me.

So back to spilling the story about the Stallion.

Cousin Luke was nobody's cousin. He had been in the Temecula area for as
long as anyone could remember. He wasn't too well liked. He had the face of
a goat and that weird flakey skin. Some ignorant folks called him the hunchback.
His back was fine.

He was actually very different than the famed hunchback cause Cousin Luke was a
proud man and liked the public, it's just that the public didn't take much to him.

He was a little tough to look at. Never saw him talk to a woman except to ask
for more coffee. I saw a child starin' at him once in Bixby Park and he grabbed
the child by the ears and said sternly, with a deliberate passion, ' Look,
look, look boy! You are gazin' at the design of the heavens.' He stared at that
boy, peeled his own eyes open with his thumbs, till the toddler pissed his drawers.

The police told Cousin Luke to stay outta the main town, for the sake of the
children, but the poor son of a bitch needed certain food and arthritis medicine
so he was kinda up a crick.
Mighta led to him stealin' at night, but there was no proof.

Almost a year later a crime was committed. A woman's body
was found near the Mill and there wasn't much of a trial.
They knew who they wanted to bring down before the investigation even began.
I knew he was too weak for manglin'. I don't know. Not
much evidence. People really pulled a Jesus on this one and claimed
they knew he was the one, in their hearts.

There was about six of us invited to the hangin'. I showed up with a big stick
cause I didn't want anyone lettin' out their transgressions on this poor fella.
He sat there, resting in a cheap saddle, rope knotted behind his neck like
blonde summer braids. A statue, balancing among the sycamore limbs.

He didn't plead for justice. He had a look on his face like he had just eaten
a flavor of jellybean he had never tried before, and then he looked proud.
I think he enjoyed bein' the center of attention for once, for somethin' other
than his looks.

He looked at me as if he was sorry that I had to be there to witness what humans were capable of.

A strange thing occurred when the horse was beckoned to run
by the hangman. It didn't budge.

The other men with revolvers cracked the horse with whips and twigs.

The Stallion still did not budge. Cousin Luke's arms were bound, head covered in burlap. Chin up.

They cracked the beast's ass until dusk
waiting to see the rider's body snap and sway
but again, it would not run from under the rider.

I interrupted and reminded the gentlemen that we had not asked Cousin Luke for his final prayer.

"Are you the prayin' type, boy?" asked Jim Murphy.
Cousin Luke's chin rose higher into the air like a bride's bouquet.

"Gentlemen. I was never at home here," said Cousin Luke, "but I felt most at home when I heard other people pray...when I was outside the church. Everyone sounded scared. So no, I don't pray. Soon, I'll be close enough to God to feel the lightning in his spit, so why bother. I did write somethin' down I'd like to read to you gentlemen, but you'll have to remove this burlap, for just a spell."

Danny Hatch slowly lifted the cover with the tip of his shotgun and retrieved a letter he found in Cousin Luke's trousers. I kept it to this day. I can hear him readin' it.

"Lord, if I die an honest man
let me first be honest with you.
Men can take my life
but none shall steal my pride.

I wore your sport coat made of knives
begging the world to touch me,
telling everyone they were gifts...
and oh how I wanted to open them all up.

I never hurt nobody.
I was a machine gun jammed by the seeds in Eve's mouth.
I was a Christmas tree kicking presents into the fires of midnight.
I was a war over Colombian placebo.
I was a boxer that couldn't stop swinging at the shadows.
I was tempted, but never hurt nobody.

Temptation is a talented opponent, Lord.

My eyes were scissors etched with a yes
cutting the child from the hem of her dress.

I took her to the Mill to relieve her of child,
by her request, but I did not know how to do it right.
She told me it was easy and that she could guide me through it..
I did not have the strength in my hands to finish.
I reckon she tried on her own.

I, born in a trophy case that remained empty
I, created in the image of who?

I was born in the year of the noose.
I was born in the year of the butterfly knife.

Lord, my photo album is empty
and I am glad
no more
will have to carry it.

Lord, this heart
is a corpse.
Send the night
to come bury it. Amen."

It is a strange thing to weep in front of strangers who hate you and
don't know you. I think Luke felt that.

Jake put the bag back on Luke's head.

I took the letter from his bound hands. The men continued to crack the beast and still it would not budge. I watched the stallion's face. I looked upon the shine of its eyes. No stallion can bleed in a beating without a flinch, but that's exactly what happened.

I thought this animal was from the fields of angels and demons. They hit its ass with all they had and it wasn't moving.

The bag turned towards me. I don't know if he was smiling under there or laughing but it scared the dickens out of us and we ran. I did not look back.

A corn farmer and assistant pastor, Terry Prine came by three days later to see if anyone had claimed the horse. It was understandable cause it was a good plow horse and no one knew where it came from.

He swears he just about swallowed his tongue when he saw the man still sitting among the tree limbs,
unfed, head sheathed
moaning upon that horse.

Twilight sighed down and the pastor watched him from the trees.
The farmer claimed he watched the Luke's chin finally dip
as slow and heavy as the sunset.

The horses legs lurched forward and the body finally fell.
It swung like a lopsided pinata.

Terry swore the snap of the noose from the limb was the loudest he'd ever heard.
He said his body swung there like a pendulum
and that the horse ran faster than Roman chariots
straight into that black, crackling sky.

NINE THOUSAND, ONE HUNDRED
LIGHT YEARS AWAY

My name is Todd Anderson. T-O-D-D. I am 5 feet, 9 inches tall. I am 320 pounds. I have had sex once and it was expensive.

I work at a convenience store on 7th and Cherry in Long Beach. You can come visit.
We have more beef jerky and energy drinks than the other leading convenience stores.
We have magazines. I like the ones with bikini girls next to lowered trucks. I don't get it, but I like it. A woman's bikini area is like Cuba. It's not that I've never been there, it's just that I don't feel very welcome cause I don't speak the language.

A man without a name tag takes the leftover mags back and destroys them if they don't sell. I feel sorry for all that work put into something that no one gets to see. No one gets to know how great the thing was, or even all the various things waiting inside. No one will ever know. Trashed from the get go.

I work with an autistic guy named Jerry. He has a girlfriend. I believe him. I believe in good people. I believe in music. I don't own any records.
Actually I'm not sure how you can believe in music. I'm not sure how that works.

I drive a Datsun. It has graffiti on it. Certain gangs throw rocks at it. I don't even know what it says. Maybe it says, 'throw rocks'.

I don't lie, cheat or steal. I don't have a girlfriend. Maybe that's 'cause I don't lie.

I don't have a bike, anymore. I put a sign on it that said 'please don't steal me.' A little girl stole it. I don't think she could read.

I don't exercise. I don't like sweating. I sweat a lot. I drink Gatorade. I have their t-shirt. It says "Is it in you." That's a funny one. I wear it cause it makes Jerry laugh. And me too.

I don't eat much. I feel heavy. I do feel heavy. I don't make friends easily. I don't win. I'm not a loser, but I don't win. I mean, usually I don't, but every dog has his day. And every day has...um. Every dog has his day. My day was today.

When I first met Jerry, I used to think he was rude.

"So how old are you?"

His body jumped to attention. It was as if my question bolstered rigamortis.

"The largest birthday party ever held for an individual was for the legendary Colonel Harland Sanders on September 8, 1979 to celebrate his 89th birthday in Kentucky. 35,000 people ate chicken!"

"What the fuck?"

Now I realize that his facts are his answers. Kinda. I like it. If I ask him when he was born, he'll state some random fact about 1979. I think he's cool.

He carries around a picture of this woman. She looks normal. 20's. Kind of cute. Big mole on the cheek. Old timey glasses. The weird thing is that he keeps it in a small frame and takes it with him everywhere, clutching it like a bible.

"I think Virginia Slims go in the bottom and Newports on the top. Jerry, let me ask you somethin', you carry that picture around everywhere you go and I'm assuming that that's your girl? O.K. This might seem too personal so you don't have to answer, but do you and your girlfriend ever get it on? I'm just wondering, not to be perverted."

His face pauses for a moment like he's in the hot seat on a game show and then switches to the face of the kid that stole the cookies.

"The world's fastest oyster opening is 100 in 2 minutes set by Mike Racz in Invercargrill, New Zealand, 1990. Home of a fast motorcycle."

"I guess that means you're good in the 'ol sack, buddy? I bet you are."

He high fives me.

"The world's longest sausage stretched for 28.77 miles made by M & M Meat Shops in Ontario, Canada, 1995."

If it wasn't for him, I wouldn't still be workin' here. His heart is as big as my gut. I envy him. He's got the innocence and the courage I always wished for. I do believe in good people, but I am starting to believe that except for Jerry, they have all been raptured into Eau Claire, Wisconsin.

We get a lot of weirdos.

The guy that drops off the fountain syrup is a real piece of work. He has a ducktail for a hairdo and chews his gum so that his jaw reveals the maximum amount of smack action.

"Sup, Jerry Curl. Sup, Toady Camboady? -smack-smack-smack. How's the toadstool?"

"It's Todd."

"Sorry about that, Toady. Sign this. Whoa, who's the babe in the frame? What you don't talk, Rain Man? Whatevs."

I don't know why people wanna be like that. I'd rather be ignored. As he exits I realize there is not much compassion left in me for jerks. If I had some terminal illness, I would just go around waxing and stabbing idiots around Christmas time and then I'd drive off a cliff with Susan Sarandon or something. At least I'd feel like I accomplished something. I know what you're thinking...poor Susan Sarandon.

"Delivery guys used to be so sweet. I swear to God, Jerry. I hope that guy has a dumb life and a real painful death."

"September 19, 1981, more than 300 people were eaten by Serrasalmus, or piranha when an overloaded passenger boat capsized as it was docking at the Brazilian port of Obidos."

"I hear that."

Most of our days in the shop are spent secretly making fun of mean customers.
It's brought me close to Jerry. He's been a good example to me.
He has taught me to not blow my dough as much. I buy dumb stuff. I can't help it.
Most of my paycheck goes to magazines and lottery tickets. I never win.
Not even a dollar, can you believe that? Some people find money.
But I love playing. It's exciting. The whole idea of the thing.

The lottery reminds me of life. Some people waste their life trying
to win and then some buffoon comes along, finds one in the gutter, doesn't
even try and is set forever. It's hilarious.

"Jerry, You take two scratchers and I'll take two scratchers. I tell ya, If I had the money, I'd take a flight out of here to somewhere exotic…like Arizona. I would sit on those rocks in Sedona, those red, huge towers of boulders where they say there is a vortex and I would sit up there with a big ol' box of Gatorade and I would just sweat, I would sweat all damn day until the sun cooked away my skin, till I was skinny again, like when I was a kid. I would look so good. I will let all this hurt just sweat out of my pores and I'd leave it in that vortex and I'd pay for all of my friends…well, I'd pay for you to come visit me and we'd go to some river and feel …I dunno, light. Maybe get one of those nice, lowered trucks and just sit around waiting for the photographers and girls in bikini's from east L.A. to show up. The I'd take some steroids and get strong and I'd tell everyone off who was a jerk to me. What would you do?"

"MMmmm. The biggest burrito was 4,217 pounds and was created by El Pollo Loco, Anaheim, California, 1995."

"That sounds delicious. "

We scratched them tickets. We lost.

"Why is it whenever the devil pisses in the wind, it blows back in my face! My God! Let me win…something! Let me fucking out of this shell. Give me a fucking running start for Christ's sake! Gimme one wish that isn't wrecked. Man."

There was an awkward moment.

"I'm sorry. I've never gone off like that before."

"The worst battle in history was the 880 day siege of Leningrad by the Germans during World War 2. 1.5 million Russians died and over 100,000 bombs were dropped."

"Have you ever wished for something, Jerry?"

He let out a long slow breath.

"Yes."

I was silent. Yes? He had never said yes or no to me before in over 8 months. He grabs my hand, sets my ticket down and walks me over to the rack. He opens up a Time magazine. In the back is an advertisement for learning English as a second language. The woman holding the box is in her 20's. Kind of cute. Big mole on the cheek. Old timey glasses. It's the same picture. The same one from his frame.

He stares out over a tub of bottled Pepsi and a wall of Pemmican beef jerky. His chin lowers. He begins sniffling. I stare at the cigarettes. Either his girlfriend is a model for ESL or there is no girlfriend.

"She's not your girlfriend, is she Jerry?"

He nods his head from left to right. He is sobbing.

I say "It's O.K., man. It's O.K. I think we should tie one on."

I poured two cola-flavored Slurpees. And we sat there. I think I know what he wishes for. He begins,

"The most massive star is estimated at being 200 times greater than the mass of the sun, in the Carina Nebula. It is 9100 light years away. It is called Eta Carinae. It is also the brightest."

I feel my face collapse like a stack of plates into my hands.
Tears come creeking out of my faucets.
A customer and his wife are trying to buy some peanut butter cups.
They're staring at me from behind the counter and he says, "You all right, buddy?"

"Yea. I am. Thanks." He finally leaves. Jerry puts his arm around me and gives me a nice hug. His Slurpee is empty so he takes a sip of mine and then hands it to me.

He says, "Eta Carinae is 6.5 million times brighter than the sun, but we can't see it."

"I'm sure it's beautiful, Jerry. I wish we could see it."

from **IF LOVIN' YOU IS WRONG,
THEN I DON'T WANT TO BE WRONG**

COMPLETING A DUMB PUZZLE

COMPLETING A DUMB PUZZLE

This poem was born out of the idea of your wrists as escape hatches and what if blood didn't come out, but rather the voice of someone you cared for telling you to not do it. Stop cutting yourself. I saw a tattoo a fan got of the word escape down the arms with a padlock. I was hoping to see a gopher.

I stare like bad television
at your dancer's form while you rest
not knowing where I belong.

I found you
the way your foot finds your other arch
when you dream on your stomach.

I have overdosed on the small pills of this farewell sleeping.
Wizzing your ahhhhhs.

I went to get my stomach pumped at the hospital d'resistance.
They found flecks of your tongue, sap from your bones, fingernail chips,
lipstick chemicals, liquid vaginal magic and a note:

Hold me with the word escape painted down your arms
and brush off the pairs of large buck teeth in the closet
and we'll run from the bed
through the wall
and charge into the earth as gophers in love

back to the dust
where we belong.

AQUANAUT

Most people don't know it is larger than the Titanic, and was later revealed that it cut an American Naval ship in two and had to let the sailors drown due to approaching U Boats. I think it's haunted. I think you're haunted.

Downtown Long Beach is a woman
packed with heavy ghosts
in heavy coats
who aches when the gulls pass through her.

She is woman, surrounding us in night fog
loosening our tourniquets with sultry mist,
healing wounds by directing embraces to the gasses of starlight.

Tonight, a telescope points toward her high-rise fingers,
spying the open windows for the last place God hid my ignition
for the last place I tangled the sex in your shadow.

Tonight, there are no knives.
No reason to pull the razorblade
out from behind the library card in your wallet.
No reason to soar from the green spine
of the Vincent Thomas bridge.
No reason to collapse
in the rusted regret dumpster
behind the Reno Room on Broadway.

Orion awaits over Avalon.

Remember how we wanted to water ski there,
all the way to the island
on the backs of the aquarium bat-rays?

And remember how I haggled the rays into it
by giving them back their stingers?

And remember how hard you kissed me
as we mounted onto their slime and leather wings?

And remember how the rays swerved us recklessly
through the Pacific oil rig pylons?

And remember how the sensation made you feel so close to death
which made us feel more alive?

We raced under wide Catalina stars
until the lights over Pine Street called us home
to a tired sailboat harbor
where masts creak and sway like a brigade of crosses
marching nowhere.

You said Let's steal the Queen Mary!
We'll watch her sweep through the August glow of red tides
Drinking in the tiny green fireflies of the sea.

I told you your kiss made me feel like Winston Churchill
and you said- powerful?
and I said- drunk.

Today the Queen is at rest-still unmoved,
rusted, boilers removed, gutted and ready to live.

I spend my days looking for anchors
plotting courses to deserted ports
attaching more telescopes to my sailboat
in hopes that I will catch that siren
combing her fingers through the shocks of hair
that falls from her head like thousands of wet rosaries.

If I spot her
will I see
the scars I left in your back—
mazes of amazement and black, frustrated passion?
Vanishing tattoos.

Slow halo-generator woman of Long Beach—
I will watch and wait for the look to return to your face—
The look you used to give as an Aquanaut close to death
Head rocked back
Eyes pinched full of twilight and drunk fantasy.

When the morning laughs out loud with big teeth,

When the asphalt smells like a melting Buddhist,

the devotion-the prayer-the heat-all you.

I know that the city holds you as one of its lost.

Lost for now—
never forever.

BLOWTORCH SONATA

If I was king of some land, I would break a bottle of champagne
against something everyday. If I christen you on
the head, you have to leave.

This night the stars hung like suicidal icicles—
bright
lynched albinos in headlights

I went solid and sneezed
fascinated
at the empty green 7-Up bottles of your eyes

I wanted the bar fight of my heart—
irrational,
to break those bottles upon us.

To christen us as battleships against.
Foolproof.
An empire of bon voyage.

PLEASED TO MEET YOU YELLOW,
MY NAME IS BLUE

After reading in Laguna Beach, a woman came up to me and said 'I liked your poem but I used to live on a farm in Wisconsin and to tell you the truth, blueberries don't float.' I said 'Well, to tell you the truth, I don't hover a few feet above the Pacific when I am sad. It's called suspension of disbelief. Get off me.' This is one of the few poems I have memorized and I recited it to couples when I used to be a gondolier.

ETERNITY GREEN

You came swiftly across the sea.
I hovered there,
thirty miles outside of Galapagos,
placed myself in the screams of rival winds.

I hovered there for years alone
feeding on everything blue,
shark fins, sea spray,
desire, memory and floating blueberries.

But you came swiftly across the sea
took away my death (though I guarded it).
Held my defeat by the neck and outsmarted it.
The ice in my breath floated before you
a crystal field of all my fears...

I was just getting used to the blueberries.

But you spun that warm ginger light.
Sent it spilling from the gold blaze of gasoline eyes.
Melted my breath.
Melted the soloist.
Melted the pumping thing inside.

You said, 'Hello Blue, my name is Yellow.'
and I said...'Wa. Wow.'

I was stricken, I was struck
I was a bad joke about a duck who was down
that no one ever laughs at—

but Yellow she laughs-she's a laugher
and she's not even drunk!
I say Yeah Yeah!
"I want to be something ridiculous and wonderful and Yellow"
She says, "Do you mean like margarine?"

No, I mean I want your firecracker smile Yellow,
I want your jacaranda kiss Yellow,
I want your timelessness
inside my eyeballs Yellow.

The way snow falls to earth,
Yellow whispers to Blue—
"Would you be Green with me forever?"

"I do I do I do... "   **93**

CAROLINA

The 82nd Airborne is always on a cycle called Division Ready Force, which basically meant we could rarely leave the base or travel at all in case of a conflict somewhere in the world. When we could we would head down to Myrtle Beach and we knew it was stupid but there wasn't much else to do. What else is this about? The view out of my window of the soldiers that left the 82nd, their jump boots were the last thing they'd toss onto the telephone wires. I would stare at them every night. The part about 'you're a champ' was actually heard when my buddy Fitzgerald was getting busy and I was on the floor of the motel room. Wouldn't you giggle a little? Don't ever say 'you're a champ' to someone during lovemaking, unless they're a prizefighter or small person. This poem is for the ladies of Myrtle Beach.

Their eyes know no Harlem.
Their hands know no Calypso.
Their hearts know no whispers
But those that the night let go.

You are Myrtle Beach girls.
Cruising the strip,
moving like horny groceries
on a bloodshot checker's conveyor belt.

Chant into girldom
with your Cyndi Lauper anthems
donning all that the malls will allow

How can we not fall as men
with your wine class of Coors Light la la.
I will Koresh your body.
I will sew your skirt into an evening Dresden.

Your chick packed anti-hoopty
with the ridiculous neon lit undercarriage—
chain-smoking the fear
of the stiff-chinned Raleigh boys on the corner.
Waffle House accents, homophobic jeans,
and Abercrombie haircuts.
They don't have a chance against the camisole heart attack.

The gals are hungry to ride the backs of motorbikes in mini-skirts,
the u-u-umbling engine teasing them into moist devil's dew cake.

The hot wind of Anais Nin
racing lines up their now snail-glossed legs.

You will not love him.
You will embrace him out of fear, excited.
You will cry out into the hotel night near the bathtubs full of ice,
"You're a champ! You're a nameless champ."

I found a pair of panties in the streets of Myrtle Beach.
I did not turn them in to lost and found. No way.

These were not the kind of garments that just fall from luggage.
They were manna.
I carried the exceptional panties for two years—
I made people think I was somebody.

I told stories back at Ft. Bragg about how "my girl" in Myrtle
rarely writes because of her asthma and tennis elbow.
She made me carry these panties in memoriam
or she'd cut me off from her bulbous spandex tantric lust.

Slurring to the soldiers, sharing Crown Royal
we made 'chill all love' and
I of course started cracking up.
Lacking the imagination that comes from experience,
when they in what sexual position she liked it
I would say, "normal position."

At night from the drunkenness of my barracks window
with one eye closed,
I'd watch the wonderful white flares grow,
skidding into the night
over the jump boots hanging from stale licorice telephone wires.

I'd slow them incendiaries down.
Play them backwards.
Exit them from my mouth
feel them as a kiss from phantom war harlots.

These white flares—
that told us to avert our eyes to retain night vision—
I would soon stare into
begging the light to take me somewhere...

to the kind of black-haired faceless woman
who would toss her underwear
from a moving vehicle...

just because the night told her to.

CHERRY

The names of the dead soldiers at the end were friends of mine,
fellow soldiers who were not confirmed killed.
I think terror, true terror, is born from the feeling of helplessness.
This poem is for John Condliffe.

"C-130 rollin' down the strip
64 troopers on a one-way trip
Mission top secret, destination unknown
Don't even know if we're ever goin' home
Don't even know if we're ever goin' home"
—ARMY CADENCE

I BELONG TO A PROUD AND GLORIOUS TEAM
THE AIRBORNE—THE ARMY—MY COUNTRY
I AM CHOSEN
TO SERVE THEM WELL
UNTIL THE FINAL VICTORY
- excerpt from The U.S Army 82nd Airborne Creed

The most memorable burger I ever had:
March 23, 1995.
Damn skippy I'll never forget the taste.

C-130's, C-141's on a training day
The Great Gray Whales burn over the North Carolina sky,
300 paratroopers and the Pope Air Force Base.
A priest would come to pray over us before every jump,
bless the runway.
Prayers come heavy
like piles of unopened chutes.

He passed out 'St. Michael' necklaces to the boys:
"guardian of paratroopers.
"
The Father ended the blessing,
said if we prayed as much as we drank
there would be no war.

Some laughter.

St. Michael
St. Michael is waiting for his boys.

Here, on green ramp, we would wait to chute up—
board cargo planes to dump us into unknown drop zones
It's not just a job—it's a clever advertisement.

I VOLUNTEERED TO DO IT
KNOWING WELL THE HAZARDS OF MY CHOICE

This adventure—strapped in like a madman,
105 pounds of gear

Waiting to waddle to planes like insane penguins
in camouflage straitjacket killstuff.

I slowed down my chute inspection to pull back
observe this unknown ceremony
I saw what the German officers called "The Devils in Baggy Pants"

The unrevealed fear
The wildman face paint
The aggressive practice jumps off the dock
into the chunk chunk wood chip pile
The heroin puns as they chute up

Charlie battery singing:

"The helicopter's hoverin'
it's hoverin' overhead
it's pickin' up the wounded
and droppin' off the dead
Airbooooorne shoot, shoot shoot the sonofa bitch"

American urgency of movement.
We had spirit.

A rigger's hands move like three-card monte :

Chute on back, check.
Reserve in front, check.
Kevlar secure, check.
Weapon in place, cash.
Chemical mask on side, check.
Rucksack at knees, check.

And a nice tap toward the ammo and canteens hanging off your ass.

'You're good, Airborne.'

MY GOAL IN PEACE OR WAR IS TO SUCCEED
IN ANY MISSION OF THE DAY
OR DIE, IF NEEDS BE, IN THE TRY

I could see how that part might slip from a recruiter's speech.

DOODLE LOO DOO DOO DO
DOODLE LOO DOO DOO DOOO

The catering truck pulled up late
playing that Dixie song that came from the horn on the General Lee car.
Everyone rigged, on their backs except for me.
The envy of all.

"I want to get everyone a pop, two Twinkies, some M&Ms
and a fudge bomb for dessert..."
Cheers.
"But I only got a dollar."
Rowdy man laughter bellowed.

Smittie yelled, "You better split that shit 64 ways
or you're gonna get the bath, Cherry."

The guys with only five jumps were cherries.

The bath was a collection of filled barf bags
snuck to the man next to you
dumped on your pants one minute before the jump.
You would inevitably vomit in midair from the stench.
It's a beautiful indoctrination.

St. Michael is waiting for his boys.
When I got to the truck he only had one burger.
It was so ugly
but hunger does not know beauty.

At the beginning of the runway
A C-130 and an F-16 on an approach pattern
trying to land simultaneously
mistakenly
side by side.
Sometimes an illusion,
sometimes...

The giant C-130 wing bumps the small F-16
and sends the fighter spinning
toward the earth.
An unconscious diver
limp and spinning.
I could see these two little specks
eject—eject—eject—
All the statues of St. Michael.
and nothing to control the wreckage.

It came
like a meteor
like a ball of tinfoil
you sprayed with your momma's hairspray
and lit on fire.

The raging color and demon sound of sirens melting.
A drag racer's fuel and steel spitting into the stands.

I was safe
but the men on Green Ramp could not escape
could not run
strapped down
restrained
bound by the weight of their oath
certain screaming scrambling on their backs
"Run, you sons of bitches. Run!"

With speed
you could quick release your gear in 12 seconds.
They had 10.

The way they laid there,
faces of surrender.

PFC Stephen Addington—
shotgunned Old Milwaukee beer and knew plants
Sergeant Jimenez—
drove a Camaro from upstate with no seatbelts
Private Aaron Fitzgerald—
found his wife in Korea and missed California
Staff Sergeant Jaime Interdonato—
still had 2 pinhole scars from his mother punching in his bloodwings.
Specialist Roberto Sanchez—
couldn't dance sober
Private Jeffrey Farkas—
would mute the T.V. and invent the words
Corporal Mike "Smittie' Smith—
the tightest hook shot since Kareem.

I stood there.
I stood.
Hands at my side,
squeezing the burger
unable to move.

The rabid, meteoric, howling metal
ghosting them one by one
I just stood there.

All the statues of St. Michael.

WHY AMELIA EARHEART WANTED TO VANISH

This is one of my favorite poems because Amelia is one of my favorite people ever to have graced the sky. I heard she had her first flight as a youth here in Long Beach. She was kind of manly and severely beautiful and I would stare at her on the ceiling of the boat I lived on before falling asleep.

Amelia asks for forgiveness,
looks down at the table like we are playing chess.

The larger pout of her bottom lip is imported from
Uruguay: Ooo—doo—guy.
Her R's and the A's become dizzy ghosts when she says it.

Distance.

The bottom lip
simple as a sentence.
But the upper lip,
a complex creature.

Amelia's youth-suitcased in the upper lip-ready for wrinkles.
Lipstuck lipstick lipstock residue in flushed hue
like she'd been kissing madly,
like she walked off the set of an MGM ending
cast to kiss sailors ready to die.

Some are ready to die.

Her hair looks as if she'd been running with a man in black and white
through the sets of dangerous cities.

Her few hard lines are just symptoms of sleeping on her face,
Amelia ruins pillowcases with her lipstick.

Zip focus into the darkness where her lips should meet.
God, Those corners.

The black pockets-empty and full
like poverty.

These are not simple.
Endless. Hungry. Surrounded.
Dragging air like jets of the atmosphere.
Drawing it in
in slow motion,
drawing it in freehand
into those corner lip pockets.
The separations open and close
move elastic in melody with her chest.
1,2,3,4, 1,2,3,4 1...

Air marches in
and then nothing more marches out.

I could low-crawl inside those corner pockets,
grab her gums
see if they're bleeding
to see if she wondered if she said the right thing,
to see if there was some sign of wonder or weakness or nervous,
the way dogs watch you after they've been hit by cars.

A sign that speaks of all normal persons having fear,
a bite in the cheek-a grind in the crowns
something that will give her away...
"C'mon Amelia. Come on. This is not chess, Amelia."

She says "Shh. Save your yelling for sex and riots."

Peeking at the daylight from the corners of her mouth.
The dryness chaps.
I look for bats
or sailors' initials
but nothing.

For now it is dead in here.
The fifth of July.
January second,
December twenty sixth, etc.

I wait under the quilt of her tongue.

Unthawed.

Searching for blood.

Carving letters on her canines.

"Amelia. If you leave, don't you ever come back."

Alone in the cockpit, her propellers began to spin.

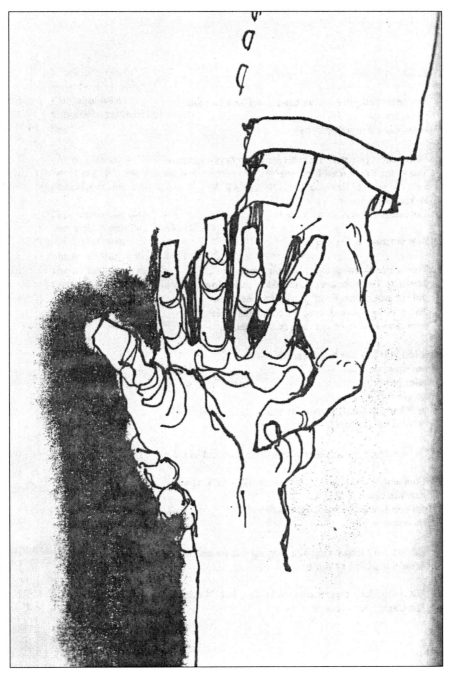

12:55

12:55

This poem was inspired by the make-up I saw on a hand at a wake. I don't think many ever got the idea that clock hands at the 12:55 position look like hands raised toward God. It doesn't matter.

You never thought a human hand could look like this.
Desert cracks.
Folds brought together by age .

Your fingertips slide across this fortune teller's nightmare.
You notice the bruised knuckles from the years he drove his fists into the walls looking for answers.

The hands of a captain who lost the entire sea.

Now the smell enters you:

The air conditioning ducts pumping medicine,
The people of white aprons, their shoulders raised from the cold
and the motionless silver goodnight machines.

The cold, the white aprons, the blood and tools,
reminders of science class and butcher shops

It hits you that this building
this room
was someone's last
toilet handle
last pillow
their last press on the power button
of a faded black remote control

You feel sorry for the nurse that lost the draw and had to make the call;

"You must come now. The doctor says 1-2 days tops."

You lean down.
His eyes haunt and float between two worlds .
He is your father,

and you can't stop seeing him carrying you on his back
through the blink of youth.

"I'd take ya for a piggyback ride kiddo...but I think it would kill me."
You laugh. He coughs. You wait.

His eyebrows lift.
They are your eyebrows
Head tilts to see your face,
"Ya know, if there's one thing I wish I would've done in my life,
I wish I would've spent more time at the office, for you."

"Really, Dad?"

"Of course not, you moron. Don't be so moronic...
Drink your coffee son. Don't waste it. "

"You got me, Pop."

"Well, it's about time."

The clock hands at 12:55 A.M. look like they're surrendering
and you think to yourself—
'This is bad coffee. My God, probably the worst.
How can they give him this shit?
Don't they know who he is?'

You drink it cause you get to drink together
and you hold his hand
wondering if anyone would notice
if you took him from this place

on your back.

THE DECLARATION OF INTERDEPENDENCE

There is this odd, black splotch on my back about the size of Gorbachev's birthmark. I look forward to having a wife someday to paint over it. This was written for my best friend Buzzy and his bride Beth's wedding. They are inspiring because the kids in them will not die. They had a kid and named him Captain. Nice.

There is a portion of my back that is very dirty
I just—can't—reach—it
I want to.
I'm incapable by design
Sheesh

Married people have very clean backs.
The education of cleansing each other.

The lover is now taught kissing as listening.
Laughter follows her flowing eye black make-up.
The voices echoing around the embrace.
Everyone in love is slippery.

And the water beats the back of your brain, girl.
You are silent with your head to his breast
searching for the heartbeat.
You hear something spinning in his torso
You hear horses wandering
A double feature of Black Beauty with Black Stallion.
Yes the book onscreen, and the text scrolls for hours
and you tell him that he carries you
and that your love is a private novel
others will not be able to turn into a movie.

The book is better than the movie.

With his vocal chords finally at rest
You hear your voice in there
narrating a life inside him.

Now the broken down water heater is coughing
The caramel lightbulb can only whisper…
'Ya'all 'r broke.'

In the dark gray sparkling steam
lids close and you see something you never saw
when your eyes were open:

The breath spilling like heavy French fog over her lower lip.
His tight fever arms gliding around her ribs.
The calm chorus in the clearing of her throat.
The volumes of yes in her eyes.
The room expanding with his every sigh.

The FBI are thankful they decided to tap your walls.
They jot down the undocumented facts
about the suspicious power of poor people
breathing naked
in a hard water love
soaped in the arms of senseless trust
and silly silly.

They jot down other things which are of course, classified.
Filed under Union Shampoo.

These unions:
Stars and Travelers.
God and Mystery.
Cheech and Chong.

The details.

The details make us whole.

Our worlds are dizzy giggle spinning carousels
that get shut down, cobwebbed and quiet
and we can't find the controls to get the thing running again.

Dirty crooked broken yesterday machines wasting.

I dream of a being cleaned, of
being clung to.

So hoorah for the unions
that give birth to curious children inside.

And tonight we release the children
and we'll watch the children run to the carousel
ripping back the dusty cloaks from their favorite painted creatures
like wee matadors.

Hey, there's a crimson-and-green-striped dragon with a twisty gold mustache!
There's a Neptune Blue seahorse with a magenta smile like your mamas juice!
There's a gypsy angel in a marigold dress with wild voyaged eyes,
and the black horse...the black horse is for you.

The kids grab the rails and run this carousel into momentum
set it spinning with force
and if this merry-go-round spins our children fast enough
you will feel alive enough to forget yesterday
and you will call the horses, horsies
and yell to them for more speed
until it rips faster and faster
snapping from the base
spinning into space

and the children giggle and listen to the earth under them
and realize
that some broken-down machines
can always spin again.

SPEAKING 12:55 INTO THE STUPID COMPUTER DEVICE

This was a strange experiment that really freaked me out regarding the philosophy that losing control reveals truth in writing. I spoke the 12:55 poem into a computer recorder with an introduction and this is what came out. The computer made parts of it more beautiful. Hello future.

all vacuum girl's name was princess
she was biggest status dope used
princess of all
she wore tight hands and the voice used to collar in
the hand wool
doesn't make me a speech

he has it
and for that I resent it

a cheat it should scratch it should it to

we work not only to produce
but to give value to time
you never thought human hand could look like this desert cracks

folds brought together by age of fortune tellers night your fingertips

slide across these haunted valleys of rail

familiar now the smell enters you the AC docks to us duck duct
the AC ducts pumping medicine bow
rubbing alcohol dead machines

you feel sorry for the nurse that lost the drawing
had to make the call
you must come now
quote the doctor

says he has wanted today's tops
the doctor says he has won to two days tops

you lean down he is your father and you can't stop seeing him caring you aren't his back through the blink of youth

I'd like to take it for the Quebec Wright K-ato but I think. it did kill me

you laugh he costs you wait to now is the chance
to say something important to your father
would take telescope to find the right words

his eyebrows lift is his head tilts to see your face
you know if there is one thing I wish I would've done in my life I wish
I would've spent more time at the fast
are really debt out about it to do that

the book about the ice ureters in the city that its a shine and sooner
and move to be stupid no

drink your coffee treated all in one

should wasted by 1/8 into the waste the clock and to 155 a.m.

look like their surrender and now he figures of this
is that county probably worse come coffee North America

the duty to annual the owners in

one would notice
it took him from his pace
on your back.

ANGELS THAT LEAK

I love film noir movies like Sunset Boulevard, Double Indemnity and The Lady From Shanghai. This was spawned out of that feel. I'm kind of a scrawny guy but this really happened.

So what do you like most about me?

Most? Hmmm. That dress. I like that dress more than anything.

As the man finished saying this, the woman reached up to her smooth shoulders, shifted thin straps of her dress to her triceps and straightened her arms slowly like a soldier on medication. The dress fell to her feet, silk accordions.

She stepped from it, struggling with the trap of her heels and stayed still. The man retrieved the dress from the dirty carpet, swung it upon his forearm and said nothing as he turned for the door. Her original body, stiff and cold. She didn't expect that.

The man closed the door behind him. He could hear the swash of her legs, skin against skin. Maybe she sat down to weep or read. The man counted to thirteen, ten being too predictable, and kicked open her door with the awkward force of a thousand rookie detectives and charged in. Smash clank of his shoe above her doorknob. She inhaled her scream, tried to cover herself but it was too late. Their bodies pounded around the room. Cherry candles vanishing from the heat, rips in the wallpaper, couches torn down to their skeletons.

This was only the way they kissed.
Wall to wall,
with a dress smoldering on the lampshade.

ALICIA'S SCIENCE VOLUNTEER

This poem got so weird, I just started chopping it down to what you see here.
Oh and this woman did have really deep, beautiful ankles. I was crazed about her.

If being a small poodle means
I can lap milk
from that soft and nameless curvy dish of skin
behind your ankle
while you sleep,
then yes,
you may put me in the machine.

SEVEN YEARS TO DIGEST GUM

There is a real dirtiness to this poem. It was written at a time when I wondered if it was really possible for man to invent lust or if God put it in us to watch what we do with a war like that. It was also inspired when I caught two shoplifting girls when I worked at a magic shop. The looks on their faces as they looked for receipts in their pockets that were never there stays with me. This was written while listening to the Afghan Whigs.

I have your gold, honey humper
And guess what?

I swallowed it
'cause I read a book about internalizing self worth.
It said to keep something terrible inside me.
I swallowed your cool liquid gold.

It's dripping off my chin.
You want it?
Come and get it.

You want the dogs?
I'll cut 'em loose.
I've got a soundtrack of dogs crawling on their bellies.

The book said to build molds of beautiful marble hands
so you can practice letting them go.
It said to drop them off of buildings
and record the sound they make failing through the air

Sound is something we can hold onto.

Woman D6 chews gum in bed—
swallows it and talks of bad luck.
She says I lay in bed like a fallen statue.
Older women have taught me to hold still.

The rain tins down.
The grass will get so tall.
The dogs need a place to hide—
pretty dogs.

Her hovering screen-door-colored skin drapes me,
shadows melt down the wall,
we kiss in Spanish,
nothing is understood.

She has ascended,
trapped with the spine of her spirit
pressed to the roof.

An angel in amber
pulled by the warm steady light
the color of flat ginger soda.

Pulled deep within my brain
You find my soundtracks.

I have a soundtrack of shoplifters
looking for their receipts.

I have a soundtrack of young women's throats
clearing in dressing rooms.

I have a soundtrack of bored jurors
thinking sex,
crossing uncrossing pantyhose across pantyhose.

I have a soundtrack of innocent men
hanging by their necks,
kicking their legs denim across denim.

I have a soundtrack of predators
caressing the hands of their prey.

I got a soundtrack of dogs
crawling on their bellies
low in the grass
moving towards the bird.

A soundtrack of doors only closing.

Spines banging against the ceiling.

A soundtrack with songs learned at birth.
A soundtrack of guardian angels swallowing sleeping pills.
A soundtrack of drool-slithering, creeping hounds.
A very catchy song
in a very catchy loop.

A soundtrack playing on the needles of our instincts
rotating
in every miserable, merciless beast.

A FEW THINGS YOU PROBABLY ALREADY KNEW ABOUT EMUS

A FEW THINGS YOU PROBABLY
ALREADY KNEW ABOUT EMUS

This is one of those poems that was written while it was happening. It's a bit like a journal due to the little pink notepad I carried around in that unique nation known as Texas. I rarely read this at shows 'cause my father lost three people he loved soon after this was printed. If he ever does read this, he should call me.

On the flight into Houston,
children sitting behind me realize that many words rhyme with
turkey.
"Look, it's a flying turkey
No, it's a flying Turkey Murky Jerky!
No, it's a flying Murky Jerky Perky Lurky
Hurky Gurky Durky Quirky Furky Turkey,"
I feel the Bloody Mary sizzling inside me.

Kids—What you're seeing is just an airplane.
What you're doing is pissing me off.
Have Daddy share some of the Ritalin he's been bogarting
before I go Monte Cristo on both of your hineys.
If you want to read or sleep, that's cool.
If you continue to irritate and rhyme all flight, I will eat you.
I will rock you, Amadeus!
I feel ill and if you don't calm down
I'll swallow both of you whole. Shhhh.

"Like Jonah."
What?
"Like Jonah in the whale?"
Sure.
"Like Jonah Mona Bona..."

They were all right kids, I guess.
They gave me something to concentrate on so I wouldn't vomit.
If only they knew I was concentrating on severing their tiny hearts.
Bye kids, take it easy.
We're kids, we always take it easy!

My father and stepmother Judy picked me up.
Tractor and trucking hats,
mesh and already sweaty.
A gift for the city boy.

119

I go to hug him.
I can tell it is a foreign move.
I squeeze even harder.
It's been two years since I've even touched him.
It's been 29 years since we've spoken.
Really spoken.

I heard the doctor spanked me good when I was born.
My dad knocked him out
and Pop held me in midair, without smiling,
without speaking.

I think this was the last time he held me.

His "Hello, I missed you" comes out as a hearty "Let's eat!"

Texas is one big buffet.
I watch the old me sneak Budweiser cans into the dining area.
They slip their cans from the secret pocket of their Sears overalls
And slowly open the tabs as if they were defusing bombs.

I got back for seconds.
Fried catfish.
Fried okra.
Fried rice and for an ethnic flair,
French fries!
Even the milk was fried.

Father lights a cigarette in my face. My chicken tastes like menthols.
We leave.

At my Father's trailer, there is a hired hand named Bob.
Bob went to the Nam.
Bob says "Navy nurse broke off a needle in my hip, for spite.
I did not like it."

You didn't?

"No, I didn't, but I threw my full bedpan at her, for spite."

Bob is addicted to alcohol.
Bob likes to draw.
Bob has Agent Orange.
Bob knows he's not very good at drawing.
Bob still draws.

A few things you didn't know about emus! :

1. Best to kill and eat at 14 months.

2. Hard to take their eggs at night. My Stepmother Judy has 20 stitches to prove it.

3. Natives of Australia. Dad says "Aboriginals used them for centuries."
I ask him if the ab-originals were the first people to do sit-ups.
He smiles.

4. 50,000 currently in the U.S. Dad says pretty soon they'll take over,
Like the Mexicans. It's not meant in a racist way.

5. Their oils can make you better looking.

6. Tastes like beef.

Mowing lawns in Texas is much different than mowing lawns
on the sun, but only because
there is much more beer involved.

Bob actually fell off of his mower and accidentally
mowed a chicken.

My father was upset, not because something living had died,
he was upset because something he had paid for was gone.

Am I still talking about chicken?

Texas makes you know God resides among air conditioning.

My father won't buy air conditioning but has a three-thousand-dollar
satellite dish.

Judy asked me if I'd like to go to the supermarket.
I went for the AC.
The air in the store smelled like Antarctic blowjobs
and produce. Ahhhhh.

In the checkout line-an elderly woman stands behind me
with a jug of punch.
I asked her where the wild party was.
She told me that her partying is like a dog chasin' a car, getting' hit,
and still not knowin' how to drive.

I told her that if she wasn't a poet, she should be,
because I had no idea what the hell she was talking about.

When we come in from the market
I handed him his beers.
handed me old Black Cat firecrackers.
We went outside.
I waited for the burden of conversation to come.
We pretty much just drank.
I almost blew off my thumb.
I kept the fireworks exploding in case he could hear what I was thinking.
I wish I could forgive you—POW!
I wish there was no regret—POW!
I wish I could forgive you—POW!
You messed up—POW!

He breaks the rhythm:

"At one time, I had seven whores livin in my trailer park. One woulda
been good for you. Little chubby, but she got a good future as a
dental assistant, even got her a new little Hyundai,
was doin' great, till she got on the hashish."

This was the deepest of our and I still had not said much.

If you lose a remote control in Texas the channel will never change!
It is much to hot to be movin' around like a maniac, changin' channels and all.
Madness.

"This is C-Span."
Silence.
"Do you like C-Span?"
Not in particular.
"Well, why are you watching it?"
Lost the remote.
"Well, I can get up and change it..."
Now don't go acting like a maniac. I'm relaxing.

Later, he shows me how to use a power saw and tells me
when was 23, he had to jump from a burning building
in San Francisco.
When he got to the fire escape, the people were yelling jump—
And there was nothing to jump into.
This happened when I hugged him.
Jump Jump Jump!
He still doesn't trust people.

"We honeymooned in Las Vegas, your real mother and me.
her to get away from the blackjack table cause she was bringin'
me bad luck."

He looks at me like I'm supposed to laugh
but its much too funny to laugh.

Pow.

My father's words drop like white noise.

I let the dusk colors fall into me:
The seeping blue-eyed hunger of a faithful starving dog
Fat garlic mosquitoes
The boredom clouds of the hottest gray.
Sapphire sky shifts and the tall green blades sway, deep.

At the fourth of July picnic
Uncle Cecil broke out his .22
and starts a genocide for snapping turtles
pulled from the pond.

My cousin Tom threw me in the pond and my watch stopped.
I believe my watch stopped when I crossed into this state.

Every Church is a time Machine.
I visited a Church of Christ a few days earlier.
They don't believe in music
because the Bible doesn't say to have music.
My cousin Tom said, "The Bible doesn't say to wipe your crack,
but you still do!"
He gets a little preachy sometimes.

Tom tells me that Uncle Cecil doesn't come outside much
anymore.

Three years ago he watched his friend die in his arms
from a bee sting.
A damn bee sting.
The doctors told Cecil all he could've done to save him was to
break a pen in half and insert it into the front of his neck.
At the right spot he could've breathed again.
It sounds too dangerous to try and he just didn't know.
Cecil sure as hell knows how to do that now.
That kinda stuff happens in Texas.

It's hard to fall asleep in Texas.
The air is feisty
thickens your blood,
I drink beers to fall asleep
Dad says Goodnight son, if we all die tomorrow,
at least you know I'm happy.

This scares me in a Jim Jones kinda way.

I turn the TV on through the night
I leave it on a squiggly channel
for artistic reasons.

My stepmother wakes me by telling me
It's hotter than horny hogs in Hell's jalapeno hot tub.
She's right.

Judy pours herself some orange drink—
Cancer makes Coca-Cola taste crummy now.
She sure drinks a lot of it.

She says "Do you wanna go to the mall? They got everything.
Let's roll!"
I ask the lady in the 99¢ store how much the rings costs.
She says 99¢.
I asked for any kind of interesting ring for my stepmother.
She slid me a pewter one of two people humping.
I said, "Interesting."

We roll down the windows on the way home.
The wind rips the scarf from Judy's head
She grabs up and
Screams
and we swer—v—e,
almost into a ditch
Look out!
My scarf!
Take—e the wheel—God—jeeeeez!
We breathe.

She said she didn't want me to see her like that.
I tell her that many women movie stars in L.A.
shave their heads on purpose and I think it's pretty cool.
She says really, like she was four and I had told her about Santa.

I felt sorry for my stepmother Judy,
not because of the cancer, but because of what her ring meant.
I wanted to replace it with my silly one.
She drives home kinda dangerous, as well she should.

It's hard to sleep again tonight.
Exotic dancers on T.V. are never down and never call.
As the beer makes me sleepy
I step outside
and stare at my watch
I piss into the 2:00 AM
and the forgiveness still waits inside my watch.

The trees outside here look dangerous.
Too dangerous.

I wish I could forgive you
I wish there was no regret
I wish I could forgive you
I already said that.

125

JOIN THE AIRBORNE

I thought I would die during this time in my life.
It really made me glad to be alive after that.
I would like to talk to anyone thinking of joining. There is pride for the living.
And honor for the ones who don't make it.
Your Mother doesn't care about honor.

I asked why our foxholes needed to be so deep.
"When an enemy grenade lands in the foxhole that you dug six feet deep, the shrapnel will not destroy any men or equipment. When the enemy sends a ball of fire through your fat head, we don't have to worry about burying your sorry ass cause you've already done the work for us."

A Drill Sergeant used to tell me when he would be absent so the squad leaders could beat up the 'ate up' privates. We beat up a guy who wet his bed before inspection. His name was Middleton, I think.

Going for weeks without even seeing a real woman
makes you want to kill even more.

A new paratrooper caught the wind into the training tower. His chute collapsed and he straddled the metal. Eighty feet up, he wept in pain and we joked about his balls cause there was nothing else we could do.

During basic training, a friend from L.A. in my unit tried to kill himself by trimming his dog tags and jamming them into a light socket. I forget his name. Maybe Stone.

At every base is a main flagpole with a ball on top called a truk. It contains A razorblade, a bullet and matches. It is for the commander of the base, if over-run, to climb to the top, cut up the flag, burn it and blow his brains out.

The 82nd has a marquee near Bastogne street. It has a number on it. If we could make it 82 days without a training accident we could have a day off. not because of the cancer, but because of what her ring meant.
We hadn't had a day off in 10 years.

Because of the large increase in suicides near Christmas time for members of the 82nd, the base hired a NY choreographer to do a musical based on making soldiers feel good about being alive. I was in it. We sang Memory from Cats and We Got a Lot of Livin' To Do from some play. It was ridiculous. It was one more thing we did for show. The guy that stood next to me in one of the songs I step outside hung himself to death.

Walking through airports in beret, jump boots and secrets,
I have never felt so proud.

THE FIRST TIME YOU HUGGED ME IT WAS WITH YOUR LEFT ARM

THE FIRST TIME YOU HUGGED ME IT WAS WITH YOUR LEFT ARM

I am very attracted to themes regarding dismemberment.
So is Aimee Bender so this is probably the last one I write for her.

The entire island had a warm glue-gun smell.
The air dripped honey silver moons.

One afternoon
rafting in the Pacific
my wife fell off
and stayed down for one minute.

I marveled at her lungs.

She popped back up with no arm.

(It's much more horrific in imagining it than actually being there).

I struggled and threw her back on our rented raft.
She was bleeding everywhere.

I tied her shoulder with my swimming trunk drawstring.
I watched for more sharks.

She said " Oh God. Oh My God.
I'm getting blood on your new shorts, my God, O my God."

I said, "Don't worry about it. We'll get me some new ones."

She said "How can you love a woman with no arm?"

I said,
"I probably...can't."

When I say I loved your guitar playing Aimee I meant it
and your arms around me was my reason for staying on earth.
I can't imagine you throwing your arm around me.

It is the truth
so be quiet and rest here.
I'm going to get out and drown to death.
You'll float to shore soon.
I know you're shaking
but hush it.

Make my last...half embrace a good one.

It was the arms I loved.
It was your arms that I needed.

The man laid near her gushing shoulder for a moment
covered himself in her life
and vanished into the deep.

TOMB

*Someone read this poem of mine and asked if it could be printed on a huge poster
and put in a storefront window in Long Beach. It seems to take on a new meaning
when the text is big. In a book it seems to mean that love is war and do everything
you can to taste it at least once. Huge, it seems to say war is not worth dying for. I
think man understands war innately, but not love. I think war is necessary as long
as people keep failing their speech communications classes.
Here it is. make it what you want.*

THE GREAT BATTLE

love is the only war worth dying for

A FINGER, TWO DOTS, THEN ME

I guess people love this poem the most. Maybe cause it explains what happens to us when we die in a way that might seem possible. Actually, I have no idea why this one is the most popular. This was written after I had read an article about a father who laid out a blanket for himself and his son in a park by my house, then planned on killing both but after he killed his son with the shotgun, he tried to kill himself but screwed it up and lived. I wanted to coat the wickedness of that scene with something romantic and kind of funny so the park won't hold that memory for me. Beauty is born from tragedy.

A VOICE AT THE PRECESSION

132

Lying together in the park on Seventh,
our backs smoosh grass and I say
I will love you till I become a child again,
when feeding me and bathing me
is no longer romantic,
but rather necessary.

I will love you till there is no till.
Till I die.
And when that electroencephalogram shuts down, baby
that's when the real lovin' kicks in.

Forgive me for sounding selfish
but I won't be able to wait under the earth for you
(albeit a romantic thought for groundhogs,
gophers and the gooey worms)

I will not be able to wait for you...

but I will meet up with you
and here's where you will find me:
get a pen—

Hold your finger up
(two fingers if your hands are frail by now)
and count two stars directly to the left
of the North American moon.

You will find me there.

You will find me darting behind amazing quasars
Behind flirtatious winks
of bright and blasting boom stars!

Sometimes charging so far into space
the darkness goes
blue.

I will be there chasing sound waves
riding them like two-dollar pony ride horses
that have finally broken free and wild.
I will be facing backwards, lying sideways,
no hands, sidesaddle, sometimes standing
sometimes screaming zip zang zowie!

133

My God, it's good to be back in space...Where is everybody?

You will recognize my voice.
You will see the flash of a fire trail
burning off the back of me
burning like a gasoline comet kerosene sapphire.
This is my voice.

Don't look for my body or a ghost.

I'll resemble more a pilot light than a man now.

I'm sure some will see
this cobalt star white light from earth
and cast me a wish like a wonder bomb.
And I'll think "Hmmph. people still do that? Good."

I'm sure I'll take the light wonder bombs
to the point in the universe
where sound does end.

The back porch of God's summer home.

It's so quiet, you float.
It feels the way cotton candy tastes.

I say to him...why do I call you God?
He says 'Because Grand Poobah sounds ridiculous.'
(Who knew he was so witty?)
I ask him 'Lord, so many poets have tried to nail it
Ginsberg, Corso, and missed,
what is holy? What is actually holy?'

At that moment,
the planets begin to spin and awaken
and large movie screens appear on Mars, Saturn and Venus
each bearing images I have witnessed
and over each and every clip flashes the word

holy.

armadillos—holy
magic tricks—holy
cows' tongues—holy
snowballs upside the head—holy
clumsy first kisses—holy
sneaking into the movies—holy
your mother teaching you to slow dance
the fear returning
the fear overcome—holy
eating top ramen on upside-down frisbees
cause it was either buy plates or more beer—holy
beach cruiser nights—holy
the $5.00 you made in Vegas
and the $450.00 you lost—holy
the last time you were nervous holding hands—holy
feeling God at a pool hall but not church—holy
sleeping during your uncle's memorized dinner prayer—holy
losing your watch in the waves and all that signifies—holy
the day you got to really speak to your father cause the television broke—holy
the day your grandmother told you something meaningful
cause she was dying—holy

the medicine
the hope
the blood
the fear
the trust
the crush
the work
the loss
the love
the test
the birth
the end
the finale
the design
in the stars
is the same
in our hearts
the design
in the stars
is the same
in our hearts
in the rebuilt machinery of our hearts

So love, you should know what to look for
and exactly where to go...

Take your time and don't worry about getting lost.
You'll find me.
Up there, a finger and two dots away.
If you're wondering if I'll still be able to hold you
...I honestly don't know

But I do know that I could still fall for
a swish of light that comes barreling
and cascading towards me.

It will resemble your sweet definite hands.

The universe will bend.

The planets will bow,
and I will say
"Oh, there you are.
I have been waiting for you. Now we can go."

And the two pilot lights go zooooooooom
into the black construction paper night

as somewhere else
two other lovers lie down on their backs and say
"What the hell was that?"

HOW TO KISS THE BOYS AND THE GIRLS: FRENCH AND PROPER!

*When I hear lovers saying 'my lady' or 'my man,' it makes me think
that ownership is kind of a romantic notion,
especially when associated with hell and French kissing.*

1.
introduce yourself and say excuse me ma'am/ sir,
did you fall from the sky?
no, why do you ask?
because the same thing happened to my friend,
Lucifer.

2.
take her/him by the hand. make sure to interlock fingers with her, keeping
one hand free. say you will never leave her/ his side. moments after, you may
uncross the fingers on your free hand.

3.
slide your fingers across the nape of her neck, gentlemen. feel the spine.
know that it is yours.

4.
bring your lips to her neck. do not kiss. whisper a promise into her neck. keep
a straight face.

5.
true ladies, rest your hand to the center of his chest. search for a heartbeat.
disguise the look of horror that comes over you.

6.
kiss his mouth, ladies. let the tongue glide along his teeth, signaling his tongue
to meet yours. feel the shape of his canines. know that yours are greater.

7.
let her kiss fill your ear, fellas. ignore the echoes and gnashing of teeth
that whisper your little secret. they know your secrets, gents.
go pussycat. you can't overdo it. you can't undo it.

WHAT I LEARNED IN CHURCH

This poem came out of a feeling of fondness for the failures in human beings.

Grace is a child's head
buried in a pillow
or asleep in the dugout.

Grace is two lovers
hiding in the theater
as it closes.

Grace is an adult
asleep at the bar
or behind the wheel.

Hallelujah.

MISS LAKE MICHIGAN

I put on the persona of someone who had been underwater too long and driven
mad. This is what came out. Please don't sue me for the Disney reference.
On second thought, go ahead and sue me cause I am all about Knott's Berry Farm.

I miss Lake Michigan.

You were right Mona.
The mellowing process worked.
I like the white men in white.
I don't kick them in the stuff anymore.

I tell them I had a bike!
I say "Oh Mona, where is my 1973 Triumph cycle?"
Of course they don't answer.
None of them are named Mona.

I know it is loaded with rust.
I know I launched it into Lake Michigan in front of you.
It was a very humbling experience...
when you didn't dive in to save me.

I held the handlebars all the way in!
You didn't think I could.
Your ugly boyfriend didn't think I could.
You dared me, Mona.

I got so cold and I wondered if you were cold too, Mona.
The exhaust pipe kept me warm down there.
The headlight only worked for about a minute
and I tell the white men in white what I saw.

Fishing lures dangled like medals
from the strong feesh? fishes? fishies? mouth.
They trailed clear strings of 20-pound test behind them.
Bridal manes of fishing line—HAH!
That made me laugh cause everyone knows fish can't get married
unless they're arranged marriages
cause all fish are Japanese.

Down there, I saw the bodies of the mob.
Atlantis was there (just a suburb). **139**

Thingamabobs? You bet!
I saw a beautiful crab named Bruce.
He was talking to me like he had a secret. Maybe about women,
but I didn't understand.
It was all in Japanese.

It sure was neat.

I miss you Mona.
I have a dress I stole for you I still need to give you.
It's worth 600 dollars.
I think you are worth 600 dollars.

I am worth a cool 150—
Bazillion.
Can't you see that Mona?

I miss your well-flossed smile.
I miss the pictures you would tape to my hands
to remind me of the things
I used to touch.

The steel table has a pole on the side.
It feels like a handlebar.
Vrooooom.
I miss my triumph Mona.
I do.

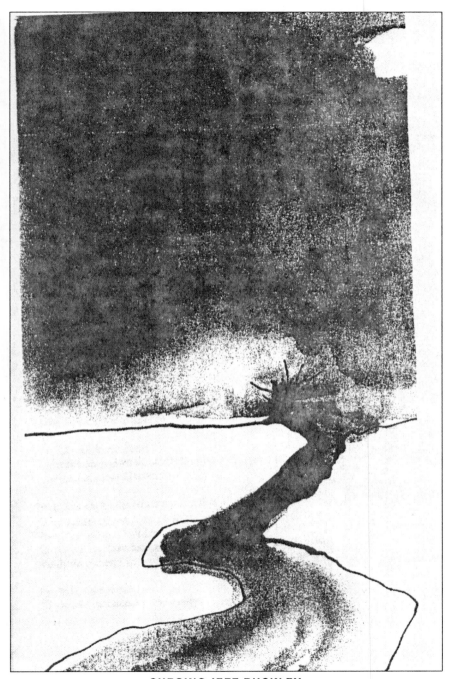

CURSING JEFF BUCKLEY

CURSING JEFF BUCKLEY

Only the deaths of Johnny Cash and Jeff Buckley made me weep. Most celebrity deaths
feel like a publicity stunt and never touch me; Jeff had so many lines about shoes
fillingup with water and nightmares by the sea.
What does it mean if your art tries to tell you how you will die?
I read this poem in Munich and the bartender took me to
the place down in the basement where Jeff had signed the wall a year or two earlier.
He let me sign right next to it and it was an honor as much as it was strange.

"I couldn't wait for the nightmare
to suck me in and pull me under, pull me under."
—SO REAL, from the album Grace
J. Buckley, three years before his drowning

You sultry poison.
You angeldust donor.
You American gunmetal tongue
stealing the power from women.

You said the nightmare sucked you in
and pulled you under.

The muck of the river filling your wide shark-toothed mouth.

You cried out into the hard Southern night
and the moon is still helpless.

You held your breath
and went down.

Young body convulsing in the brackish water
shaking for life,
moaning for the surface June bugs.

Bubbles roared from your throat
filled with swirling notes of terror—

The last melody—the most beautiful.

You said the nightmare sucked you in
and pulled you under.

You died brilliantly.

...but how did you know?

SPARKLER

I once had a girlfriend who got so upset she got out of my car so I drove off.
To me this is the best thing to do for a person who never got to experience
the joy of walking 22 miles.

Driving on a 70 mph asphalt,
my woman's voice comes out like a spit-on drive-thru speakerbox.

"We've lost focus, I feel the spark is gone.'

I look at the windshield instead of out of it.

I pull over,
remove a snow chain from the trunk,
tie it to the bumper,
let the end dangle on the blacktop.

From the driver's seat
I tell her 'For the sake of clarity
could you step from the car for a moment?'

She does.
I drive away.

She focuses on the chain and
it looks like the fourth of July.

PUSSYCAT INTERSTELLAR NAKED HOTROD MOFO LADYBUG LUSTBLASTER!

*This poem was inspired by a Sparklehorse song and a Pavement song. Hence the sparrow reference for Sparklehorse and the 66 shades of black for Pavement. 'Be cause there's 40 different shades of black, so many fortresses and ways to attack..."
Mine is 66 cause of a road trip listening to that album. Never ask your lover to write you a poem. It's like asking sperm to hurry up and be a baby.*

pussycat interstellar naked etc etc.

how silly i get.
how lost and silly i get
unravelling my fingers
to where your arms connect.

i come to your body as a tourist.
endless rolls of black and wine film in my fingertips
documenting the places that change your breathing
when touched with the patience of glaciers retreating drip by drip.
it reverses your breath back into the places
that trigger subtle curls in your purple painted toes.

the breaths are not worth hundreds of sparrows
they are worth all the gray air sparrows die and wander in

there are things about you i collect and sell to no one.
i journal them in a book you gave me with the inscription,

'don't leave your ribcage in the icicle air. something will break.'

i wrote about the courage my hand would need
aiming down the worn comfort of your hair,
hang-gliding across the summer slits of your winter dress,
searching the perfection in your rock-and-roll breasts,
stealing the heat off the drug of your stomach.

let me die a White Fang death
trembling on the snow and linen of your shoulder blades.

I want to buy you a black car
in 66 shades of black
to match the wandering walls of your heart
filled with the mysteries of space and murder in space.

let me spend my days on the shores of abalone cove island
collecting bottles that wash ashore
and burning the messages inside
to fill them with new messages like
"send more coconuts" or
"send more coconuts and wild boar repellant. i'm re-reading lord of the flies." or

"wow, I'm actually on an island. please send my five favorite albums.
I've already built a Victrola out of sand and eel poo-poo.
It's the MacGyver in me. this volleyball won't shut up."

I will float the armada of messages towards the atlantic
and wonder if a pale girl in new york spends time at the shore.

I will wonder if she can see the stars i carved our initials into
when I got sick and weightless.

lay in bryant park and look hard into the air.
your last initial isn't up there
for it is worthless to me
since I had dreamed of changing it.

this is the love of mercenaries.
i'd kill an army of sleeping cubans for the rum desires
in the clutch of your tongue.

touche to your lips!
touche to your way!
touche to your ass!

you are an electric chair disguised as a la-z-boy
and I find comfort in you.

my clear bones take shape in the mouth of glassblower with asthma
for there is no perfection in me
but maybe clarity.

crush me with the satisfaction of your black misted, unclocked breath.
I always come back to the secrets and wonder of your breath.
It is something for sparrows to wander in.

it's not that i wait for you
it's that
my arms are doors i cannot close.

QUARTER SLOTROCK

This is death when I close my eyes and speak to it until it speaks to me.
I read this onstage at the National Poetry Slam finals and took second place.
People said the parts when I was silent were more amazing than the poem.
I don't think that's a compliment, is it?

I left my wallet in the afterlife.

I am a quarter dead.
I am 75% bottled water, 24% Death Valley, and 1% 'I found a dollar.'

I sleep on my eyes and move across dream state women like a hovercraft.
I wake and my inner child has wet the bed.

I am the executive producer
telling you that most of you will die on national television,
and the bad news is that some of you will only die on cable.
That's the breaks.

I am the one man in the firing squad
who can feel that his rifle is the heavier one today.

I am the reason you need to pray.

I am the shaking in the closet that you hide from
that your mother used to call the holy ghost.

I am the fear that sexes your darkness so hard
you forget how to sweat.

I am vivid wild plastic trinity broadcasting network
in the hands of children who need to blow me up.

I am the cigarette smoking your birth certificate.

I am the tears extracted by Johnson and Johnson.
I am the blood in the fists of Mr. Charlie Bronson.
I cannot be stopped.

I am the eighty-year-old couple raptured from the dance floor.
I am their third wish
a last rite
their first kiss
just last night.

I am the rocketpack in the back of Boy's Life you could never afford.
I am the cops and fathers battering down your door
and the esteem that got stuck in the commode.

I am one man in the firing squad
and my rifle is 1.65 ounces heavier today.

I bruise from shadow boxing,
the voices that died on the sidewalks in my head
begging for more quarters
for more time in the meter.

I am the father lying over his son as the plane goes down.
I am their mothers...
I am the enemy's trigger
I am the embassy you run to
I am the bottle in the back of the cabinet
I am the space between a boot and a landmine
I am the dash in between the dates on your tombstone
I am the wind as the Injuns faced it.

I am the last thing JFK tasted.

TRIGGER AND HAPPY BELONG TOGETHER

How honest do you really want someone to be? I hope you get this feeling in your stomach at least once in your life.

If I tell you
 'you are a riot'

it doesn't mean you are funny.

When your eyes slink across me,
I get that feeling in my stomach
of a man with his new love at the pier
as she sees her old lover—
they wave to each other
and in that brief instant
you know she will never stop
missing his touch.

Love is truth
and truth comes easy
like a drill bit in the larynx.

You are a riot.

UNSENT

It's probably O.K. to tell this story since I don't know where this woman is anymore.
It's a bit too self-aware and revealing for me to love this poem.
The short of it is I cared for this female. I had a crush on her for years.
She finally started to date me. Months later she told me she was pregnant. I wept
while 'Shot in the Arm' by Wilco played. We had never had sex. It was over.

I am a relational botch job and horror trophy.
I wanted this one to go right
I don't want a relationship that simply comes together out of crisis.

Why do I care for you so much?

How bout You made me laugh like a maniac and cry like a bum.
You looked into this tinfoil chest.
I was cooking old vegetables.
I am being ripped by these looped sentences.

How could you sleep with someone you hated?

You are dating a fella whose head spins in a zillion directions.

Maybe I want to lock fingers and shut up.

I wanted into your skull to undo some sentences.

How can I measure up to the rich older fellas,
The hip art sensibilities,
when a bit of flatulation in January made me laugh through all 1998?

I goof off. I am poor. I live on a little ship.
My job isn't stable.
I have no mystery or rebellious grit.
I like dumb magic tricks, skateboards and being tackled.

When you told me about losing your virginity
do you know I wanted to be there
to shake you and say Wait dammit
wait for me.

I think of how I'd feel without you
and I am ripped into freeway trash.
I fell for you twice.
You're a big fat fuckin' wow,
so where do I belong?

You used to kiss me mean and good.
You don't anymore.
I don't know what you know about me.
I don't know what you wanna know.

I am the kinda guy who will call too much,
make mistakes on the suave scale,
say the wrong things to your friends,
play American music,
kiss you like hell.

I wanna fix what the other upstanding Christian boys wrecked.
I wanna punch out all the smart, clever
and coy billboards you dated before
and stalk all the boys with secret crushes
and places their hearts on Pungee stakes and say Suck it
she's mine.

One survivor.

I needed to flush it all out on paper.
Karate chop!
This isn't an encoded message.
This is me being as honest as I can.
You may have learned nothing from these ramblings
and Jesus... wait
I don't even know if I'll ever
show this to you.

VENTOM

I love women. Just not this one.

CONQUERED VENTOM

When a writer is wronged
in comes sweet, sweet shiv-in-the-spine revenge
in a public fashion.

You said Run like the wheelchair is calling.
Kiss hangmen cause nooses can't hold you.
Love like a leprous woman.

All of it—piss in the mouth of a Bedouin begging for water

And let's talk about our so-called sex,
the sex...Ha!
The sex...was ...was... beautiful and meaningful...but the lies!

Your vagina is a white lie.
Your vagina is Virginia spelled wrong and packed with just as much boredom.
Your vagina is a body bag for fraternity dropouts and once-hopeful fetuses.

Tear me from your lizzie borden modeling agency.
Tear me from that pink community axe wound forever.

How could you not tell me that they used to bottle your mother's saliva
and used it to taint the punch at Jonestown?

How could you not tell me her maiden name was... Beelzebub.

Your heart-colder than a necrophiliac's first entry

Your pop astrology has already made your decisions for you
Your sun is in drama
Your moon is in bullshit and an American planting his flag in you.

I could use a bear rug
with your head in its mouth
to remind me that someone else
is tasting you right now.

This is my confession
This is how I repent
This is how I pretend to be OK
in a public fashion.

The polar bear misses his eyes
but most of all—misses his insides.

Oh gosh kitty,
how long must I wait covered in lemons,
crippled in this chalk outline
unable to trust—
sour milk at every table?

I am worn like the steps to a children's mortuary.

When the poetry vending machine breaks—
all that comes is—I am so worn.

When you said you loved me so hard,
you'd kill for me,
I didn't know
it would hit
so close
to home.

from **I'M EASIER SAID THAN DONE**

THE WRINKLES UNDER LIPSTICK

Most old people don't talk to each other when they eat. What day in a relationship does that become O.K.? I'd rather drive off a cliff naked on a motorcycle than live a dead love life. No love is better than lethargic love.

There is a man
sitting across from his wife
in a senior citizens' buffet joint.
He loved fixing broken things.
She loved the garden.
He likes cornbread.
She always been partial to muffins
and neither ever knew.
His cameras zoom in on her lips
lipstick on coffee mug
on napkin
on partial muffin
on everything but her lips.

Remembering his lips painted with hers long ago
Remembering how they'd laugh when he was wearing more lipstick than she.

She only kisses the grandkids now and his mind carousels around
"...she used to..."

Creamed corn-bi-focals
Prunes-pill box
Mocha mix-lipstick
Cornbread.

He swallows and leans forward slow.
He waits until the wrinkles are ready to speak.

"When are we gonna die?"
Plates full of mistakes smeared in front of them.
She is staring at a young man to her right. "Whaddya mean we?"

The old man stands and steps outside.
He stares at nothing on the asphalt
waiting for something to happen.

A SHORT SONG

A SHORT SONG

This was a very hard day.

Lo-fi ultra sound photo sat on your lap
like a war letter to a mother
delivered by men in uniforms.

An infinite grief
wrapping your shoulders in a black mink
and dark ink.

The nauseousness left covert,
snuck from the theater of your gut, whisperless
and your new feeling of healthiness meant terrible news.

Like a lover with fists you will miss,
if you could still be sick for two more months
you would.

What do I say?

The vacancy signs of motels made you weep.

Secondary drumbeat please come in,
heaviness in your hollow.

It is a sleep that is breathless and safe.

No heartbreak, no failure, no words,
just fuzzy pictures and
the option of funeral
or leaving it at the hospital.

A doctor voicing it with the importance of fries or soup.

Maybe the child was too amazing for earth.
Maybe God is an Indian giver.
Maybe the angel of death is as fast as a bored policeman
and just as dangerous.

Now you are tested and created to carry on
to begin again.

159

You were created for creation.

You are not a morgue.
You are a factory of mud fights and beauty

and if the assembly line goes on strike
just negotiate
and things will start running again.

When the doctor told you a day before the funeral
that is was actually a girl, I know it hit you harder.
The confusion. The name change. The small clothes abandoned.
Girls seem to deserve to die less.

I watched your boys play on the cemetery trees during the ceremony.
How I wanted us to join them.

I noticed
at most funerals
the only room for an audience
is among the grass and graves
seated on plastic chairs with velvet covers
upon the sloganed tombstones of the departed flights.

I wept
sitting on a man's grave with a long name—
wondered if someday
a boy would come
sit upon mine,

not wonder about the huge way I sneezed
or kissed nervously
or idea'd my way through cashless lonely nights
inventing ways out with pens and garage-sale lights.

And when his plastic chair rickets back
he might see my name
and notice that graves are things we walk upon
and must walk away from.

If I could un-invent shoebox sized caskets
I would do this for you.

We are mist.

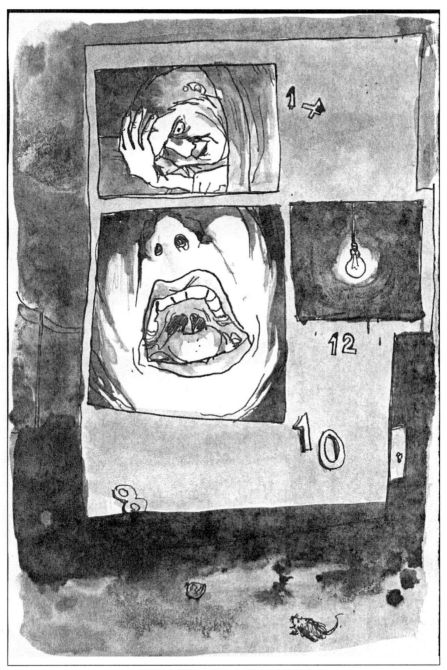

THE ABSENCE ANTHOLOGY

THE ABSENCE ANTHOLOGY

Besides living on a boat, the best place I ever lived was on the roof of Casa Grande
apartments near the Belmont Pier in Long Beach. I could see Vons and the ocean.
It was actually an old laundry room. I had to move downtown cause I couldn't
afford to live there and tour doing poetry. The woman below me would make very
jilted sounds when her older, richer lover would come visit. She was always wearing
designer gear and such. You know the type. Thirty-five or so, hungry to be married,
has to say 'I'm worth it' every time she goes shopping. It made me think about perfection.

In a bar where everything is new
but beaten up to look old,
a player piano played perfectly.

Ghosts of elephant tusks in the keys.

I wept the color of smokers' bones,
the color of night breath packed in whiskey...
Or I guess I could've just said my breath seemed orange.

I don't know what's with me these days,
the older I get
the more I try to force things to be beautiful.

The cowboy fight songs pours forth
guided by the vanished.
Some people know this feeling.

No one claps for a player piano

I stumble into the night.
Sober up hours are spent in a small Long Beach apartment
bending away the foghorn sounds launched from ocean.

The sound crawls up my stairs
like rapists on Valium.

As an interlude
I get an equal share of the young woman below me in apartment 10
begging her older lover to unRolex and turn on the water
to bless her sugar walls with the crush of Jericho
to rock her trench into something hot
codes in the 'keep trying' curve of her moans.
They are a passionate bag of chips.

I've never seen her face
but I know her moans.

Her moans are surrender,
like a coach that puts you in at the end of the season
when you've way lost.

Coach waits till the last minute to put you in
and it doesn't feel good to be in the game at that point.
It was over when you got on the field.
What you once thought you wanted you don't want anymore.

Every time she squirms or breathes out her tense sweet,
I become more alone.

My bed grows larger.
My body heat drops. Addresses vanish from napkins.
The phone line incinerates.
The foghorn slips to the ocean floor
and my only consistent company
of cars outside grows silent.

The only tail I get
is when I bet
on heads.

So I focus on the sound like the player piano and move my fingers.
Stuttering them in the air like a pianist
till her moans become music.

I turn over
and slide down the bed a bit
(which is now a quarter of a mile wide)
and aim my mouth right at hers
so we are aligned
and not in a metaphysical way.

163

I catch those sounds
brand them into my throat like a blacksmith's kiss
and memorize the nights she is alone.

The next day,
smell of diesel.

I see a moving truck outside my window.
I ask the manager why she's moving out.

He told me someone was actually moving in,
a young Marine and his Korean clean-cut wife
which is about time
since Apt. 10 had been vacant for over nine months,

partly because of the high rent,

partly because of the woman who hung herself.

CHEAP RENT

The Jewish, the Irish, the kid of the UK and the Aussies have the best senses of humor in the world. I think this poem came out of the idea that a town exists somewhere and everything is happy and fantastic, but there is a small boy locked in a cellar that must starve so that paradise can exist and have a point of reference in regards to defeat and heartache. I think I started wondering about what that boy would snack on, that is, if he was the snackin' type. Also, who doesn't imagine having a little Jew baby every now and then?

She, a strange landlord,
pointed to her chest and said
If you lived here
you'd be home by now.

I, the stranger with no deposit,
pointed to my chest and said
If you lived here
you would have to be
very…tiny.

I think of her smart hips

and the days left before their unhinging.

Our love was redder than the eyes of McCarthy.
Our love was blacklisted and strong.
Our love was a brawl in the street
with spectacles on.

Eyes of bayonet knives,
Brass-knuckle sex,
crowbar quarrels
and the nunchakus of my mouth
which I tried to use with great aplomb and theatrical flash
but always ended up knocking myself unconscious.

'No, you don't look fat in that dress.
Yes, that sentence does assume you look
fat in some dresses.'

Kapow. Right in the face.

This love remains a tongueless boy
in a basement
that you snuck graham crackers to.

He loved to see the glaze
of your hammer-and-nail-polish.
You kept him alive.
He paid you with a finger every time you arrived:

One to clean your elfish ear.
Then two
to check your pulse.
Then three
to make
an unbreakable Boy Scout oath.
Then four
for karate.
Then five
so you could rest each one
of his loose fingers in between yours
like couples do when they stroll
through shitty carnivals.

When we first met
she told me of the brilliant in Israel
and the erotic vision of the cynic.

I tried to turn her on by talking to her about
skinning animals.

She kept hunting for a metaphor.
I was actually just talking about skinning animals.

Now I can't stop thinking of how our baby would look in a perm
with massive elk for eyebrows
and then in comes the Tel Aviv
of her mouth on my dirty neck.

Our mouths building a jangly, red swamp
they will call weirdo Louisiana.

This kiss spills her silent resume:

She is the poster child
for the Willy Wonka suicide camp.

Her stomach is a summer full
of black ice-cream-truck hijackings.

Her eyes are highway fatalities
you can't stop staring at.

Her skin is rehab for sandpaper junkies.

She is my landlord
and she lowers the rent,
points to her chest and says,

"Man, if you lived here
you'd be home by now."

LAST NIGHT IN PARIS

LAST NIGHT IN PARIS

Someone told me that Paris was the city of lights when Joel Chmara and I drank
our brains out there. It was a terrible time and the boat thing actually
happened at the end of this poem. Blasted in Paris is nice.
To me it is the city of love, a sewage kind of love.
Let's just say they didn't like this poem when I read it at La Sorbonne.

For the delightful Maureen Hascoett, the last great French woman.

Say bonjour!
Say au revoir!
Say si vous plait,
or the French will hate you.

I assured my well-traveled friend
that in the City of Love
all I needed to speak was the language of love
(which is of course...English)
and they will come around.

They did not come around.

Was it the Austin bats in my jaw?
The Brooklyn fuck-you in my stride?
The Long Beach bar breath in my fists?
The South Side in my desire?
The mutt in my blood
that sent the foreign legion scrambling for American poets on the radar?

'Hu hu huuuh. Les are ruining everyzing. Les american poets are stealing all
our mademoiselles, pumping them with their inspiration, and now France is
full of ugly babies with crazy nipples. What do you do with a silver dollar nipppple!'

We will bleed all over this town
and make you think Hemingway blew his
brains out
because he had to live here for his daily intake of crazy.

We plant a flag here tonight and this-here Franceland is ours.
All you have to do is plant a flag these days.
That's why we got the whole moon and all you got is Tahiti.

Fine. Walk around all day like you just blew the Devil
and he didn't warn you when he came Hot Tamales.

You are not the city of love. I undeclare you.
I am the city of love
and we executed the mayor years ago.
Eat a bag.

Paris,
I bring you a thousand ghettos in my knuckles.
I bring you capitalism in the beginning of my name.
I bring you everything wrong about America
which tonight is inherently right.

A brigade of light
charging through your pretense.

We will walk like the boss.
We will love like janitors.
We will drink like we were just laid off.

Tourist boats pass.
Bordeaux goes down.
We yell out

'Bonjour you fuckin' Frenchies,
Here's to Scotland'…just to throw 'em off.

Au revoir.
No si vous plait.

Voices in the night.
Three cans of graffiti.
You know the colors.
You know where the stars go.

A KICK IN THE CHEST

A KICK IN THE CHEST

When I do workshops for teens, I am always amazed at their perception and the freedoms they have over most adults. This is for them and every writer clawing into something scary. Struggle makes us fantastic. Remember that.

This page is a knife to the throat
of today's poets trying to séance the '50s Beat poets
with craftless poetry,
lame snapping fingers,
bored tongues, eyes bleeding rust all over their new berets.

I cannot be that poster.
I cannot give you what you thought you might get.
I cannot give you stoner politics.
"Rasta is neither religion nor revolution
if practiced only while baked on a couch."

I cannot be a revolution dealer
pushing for applause,
inflammatory phrases with no plan of action:
'The system my friends is bringin' us down...so we should fight together now.'

But how?

'How.? Uh, that's not my job.
Let me finish this bongload and then we'll ask my third eye. Word eye. Society.'

Give their hearts action.
I will write until this mind becomes a roped-off crime scene
where failure was murdered.

How did the soap box turn into a broken polygraph?
This heart knows no yoga movement on the mountaintop of your chakras.
This heart is dredging gutters for other broken hearts.

This heart took an elevator to hell and brought you back text for souvenirs.

These shoulders are not to be cried upon for their blades cut through
tongues in cheeks.

The heart was once at peace but peace fit like a tuxedo on a red light whore.
And there are whores.
Show me a poet hungry for fame and money and I'll show you a dead actor.
I'll take a hot kiss in Hades over sex in a Mercedes.
Why?
So that if I curse the devil
my mouth can understand
the logic in the heart of the only angel denied mercy.

I want the action and the grit
and the blood inside your lips,
a knife to the throat of the poetry we knew.

It is:

A burglar breathing on your neck
stealing scenery while you sleep
and only the discarded beauty he keeps.

Like:

Hummingbirds with broken arms.
A police photo album of the suicidal breaking into heaven.
A superhero with cancer.
Boys street fighting for the feathers of dead doves.
A magazine where all the models advertise only things
that will kill you.

It's time we gave them action.
The expected is the enemy.
The plan start in the writing of that which scares you,
that which kills you.
The thing that makes you weak is the thing that makes you real.

This is for the hearts that sweat for a different kind of
muddy, scarlet, Mother, I am broken but I am still fighting kind of beauty.

Honesty is never lost in translation.

Words were our wings…
now let them be rifles.

Aim for the heart.

MILLION DOLLAR BUM

MILLION DOLLAR BUM

Bums like to attack me. I think I have that 'bum must attack' look.

When bums walk toward you,
you are glad they aren't carrying mirrors.

In a suit mauled by shovels and wind teeth.
The frittered heavy mouth of Miller's salesman speaks
Hey brother, can you spare
a million dollars?

Your guard drops like porno clothes
A million dollars?

Yes, I am a high-class bum.

I ain't got it today
Maybe tomorrow
What's your name?

Oh, my name is long and everlasting.
If I started to tell you, I couldn't stop.
But I can tell you yours for a dollar.

You nod.
He drapes the prune skin digits upon your head.
A bizarro phrenology begins.

You, son, are many sounds.
A violin played the hard way.
A heartbeat strapped to a landmine Congo.

You are the sound of walking sticks clicking in a Swiss cathedral.
When the congregation around you was blind and neutral
you ran a slide show of the Kama Sutra. Things are funny to only you.

Your name is the anthem for drunks converting
from verticalism to horizontalism
a worship song for gravity.

MILLION DOLLAR BUM

Your name is an elite circus
you often book with too many clowns
and not enough danger.

Your name is as understood as God.
He is not that awe sound.
You are not three words.

God does not speak English,
moves in feelings
among the water,
among catastrophes.
He is a feeling in your neck
that drops in your chest
and you feel like you're dying
because you are.

Your grandfather bit down too hard
on a mercury glass thermometer,
swallowed it all so the butterflies would die,
passed it into your silverquick chemistry
and you wonder why when bottles break
you are overwhelmed with a feeling of empathy.

Your name is the suppressed crisis in an anchorwoman's voice.
Your name is a wardrobe
that a lion and witch enter at a party
and say 'Don't I know you?'
Your name is
a diving board on a skyscraper.

For a name like yours,
the night never seems to get black enough,
Shotguns never shoot far enough,
Lovers never fuck fierce enough,
The bar fights never last long enough for the song to finish.

Your name is a melody that might not last long,
but listen...
Some melodies get stuck in people's heads.

BORDER STEALTH

The acclaimed California painter Jerome Gastaldi used this piece for his fantastic people of the boats campaign about immigration. Although it isn't funny, something funny did happen when I read it at the Buddhist University known as the Soka University with George Clinton, the Godfather of Funk. There was free strange cheese. George is a cool guy that has an entourage of people in white follow him around. After many glasses, we got our picture taken together by the paper and I finally got to say something to him. With a plate of cheese in my hand I said, "George, does this cheese smell funky to you?" No response. That will probably be the last time we talk. This poem is for all the students of Venice High who have turned to writing as a savior. Especially Jorge.

Son,
there is kerosene flowing over the steady drums inside me.

It was time to change our destiny.
My hands could beat that ground no further
Generations of our family turning soil reminded men like me
of what they are,
not what they can be.
My chin is lead with misery.

I would rather take it with me into the earth
than pass it down to you
Hope hones patterns in your eyes
It will not go to waste.
This is why I had to leave you.

Son,
So that your children may not live in a house of broken radials;
So that your children may not wear their skin out
in someone else's fields;
So that your children's dreams are not packed with skulls;
We die in the embarrassment of refrigerated lobster trucks.
We die in the January steam of booby-trapped tunnels.
We die in the trunk of a coyote's abandoned Honda.
We die in the onyx blackness of cargo containers where fear waits
like a tongue on a cutting board.
We die in the barbed wire that surrounds us
like the thorns of Christ.

Son,
I am a hummingbird's wing welded to your heart,
for you may never see me
but know that I am moving within you.

Our people are moving
the way the smoke surrenders to the sky
from village piles of burning tires.

Close your mother's eyes.
See me when you bleed
in the slow crimson we share flowing
down down your soil-stained arms.

See me when you are tired of suffering
in the orange fields of summer.
See me when it is your time to run.

Son,
I have not forgotten you. I have not forgotten our home,
But someday you might stand upon the shores of a better place,
pieces of salt bleached ponchos, wicker hats,
suitcases with hope's fingerprints embedded in the handles
will wash to you,
A museum bouncing in the tide,
laced in barnacles.
Brothers whose dreams were too heavy to float,
Sisters too serious to turn back,
too hungry to wait.

When you hear of some of us falling,
some of your friends will say they failed
but if our brothers and sisters fall
they have still found escape.

For in a greater way
they made it,
for exhaustion is a passport to God.

Glorious collapse is a passport to God.

A trained bullet in your back while running
is a passport to God.

CAPTAIN CREAMS

Strippers invariably hate my poetry and many of them have butt rashes. Did I get in an argument with a stripper in lovely Austin, Texas after I read this? Yes. Did I try to tell her the poem to me was about happiness and not mutilated stripping? Yes. Did she say I put an itch in her ass meaning I was a jerk? Yes. I hope it puts an itch in your ass too.

I am a stripper with no arms.

I had fake arms but as everyone knows
strippers are very against fake stuff.

I tried the pole thing and almost waxed myself.

They built me a handicap ramp. I am not sure why.
I can walk just fine.

Happiness is a dollar bill.
True happiness though
is a five-dollar bill
and they are waving it in my face.

I try to point at them to put their happiness in my underwear
but pointing is hard.

People pay a lot of happiness for these expensive drinks and dances.

Sometimes the dollar bills
have retractable strings attached to them.

Man, that's funny.
Except for the paper cuts.

Sometimes the g-string is empty
and my sense of smell is gregariously acute.
You know how when you lose your sight you get better hearing,
same thing. I lost my arms and now
I can smell like a motherfucker.

I just sit around and smell the others girls' happiness backstage.

The other strippers hug me goodnight and I just stand there
and lean in a little
doing my best.
I make a little 'hmph' sound.
I say 'Can I have some of your happiness? You pretty girls were given a lot.'
They say 'No one can give you happiness. You have to earn it, and that means
shakin' yo naked little ass a whole bunch.'

Some wave goodbye and I always say,
'Smartass.'

THE RISE AND FALL OF JULIUS WALKER

This prose poem was written right after I witnessed a terrible car accident. Outside of the Red Room in my hometown a man on many drugs rammed into a car of girls with his car, drove into oncoming traffic and nailed another car head on. His life was ruined right when I heard that explosion of steel. I felt no remorse for him. I grabbed my camera and ran to his car so he couldn't run from the cops. Later, when writing, I put on his persona and things got weird.

Four drinks ago you were cute.
Now you're a real Lauren Bacall, but blurry.
Congratulations on the promotion.
I'll say it to your face.
You're gorgeous. You're still gorgeous.

If I wasn't such a neat freak I'd shove one of my wrecked, warty hands up your boyfriend's ass and make him say it. I'd make him say it like this:

You're gorgeous and I am not just saying that because of the amazing puppetry currently engaged inside my 'dumptruck.' Gorgeous like it-hurts-to-pee
gorgeous. I see why Bert and Ernie smile so much.

You are gorgeous.
I'll say it into this glass until myself and this bar are empty.
I'll put my faith in the abilities of slow radio waves and know that somehow the message will
travel to you.
You were beautiful when you were with me.
You are gorgeous without me.
I'll hope the sound of my voice no longer reminds you of anything.
No more shall we perish. I'll pass you on with grace to him.
The sloppy kind.

The room is full of noises.
I hear the clink of glasses.
I hear the sound of secrets
in everyone that passes.
That's gonna be a song.

This bar is packed with real sport for I am drinking Jägermeister and that means Master Hunter.
I am drinking too much in a dark bar in a dark part of Dark Angeles.

You could be right here, where I am standing, in this shitty lighting, in this…everything is really red.

Now one last shot and…

The walls of this bar are melting into black. A theater.
A community theater.

We're all here to see a short play about my life called The Rise and Fall of Julius Walker.
Clap.
Go ahead.
Give it up, as they say in the hood's local color.

The programs for tonight's event are just blank bar napkins 'cause some of this stuff didn't get the morphing memo. So patrons-I would like to begin tonight's performance by sending out a sincere thank you for not going to the movies.

Look at this shit hole. How irritating is it that I couldn't summon up anything more fitting than a 99-seat theater? How terrifying, that a play about my life is a short play… with bad actors.

There is a gay guy trying to pull off being me and he is excellent,
which raises many questions.
Backstage I have switched the candy glass bottle
for a real bottle and he busts it over his head in the
scene where he tries to erase the daylight
His Mom comes in impersonating a piñata.

That's me not wanting to wake up ever again. A woman in the audience says:

"It seems so real."

The bottle part is my favorite. After the contact, the actor is bleeding and collapses 'cause he is weak! That's obvious improvising, you Method bastard! The sound guy cues my heartbeat and it makes the lights go dim. Bad power, small theater and a lead that couldn't act his way out of a douche bag, great.

Two-bit parts begin their scene. I was reluctant to hire Peter Falk but he promised to be less Columboey in this role by shortening his trench coat and no cigar. Christopher Walken is the hooker with a heart of darkness. He is supposed to represent my sense of manhood. He is holding a small TV and a picture of my mother. Peter Falk is fumbling with a dirt clod representing myfather.

Action.

COLUMBO: It seems here, da boy has a case of perplexnia, whereas when da first party witnesses da third party from da first part, he is pulled to da memory in a state of confusion on his knees like da girl was some sort of...

WALKEN: Mecca or you know...like a de-vice or a mag-net de-vice that attracts metal to the mag-net, as mag-nets do.

COLUMBO: Right. So when da boy enters da bar wit da heavy heart...

WALKEN: Can you say THE once in a-while ple-ase, old man. THE bar. THE boy. Thhh. You're making me crazy-ish. You're like bad hip hop.

COLUMBO: Hiccup? What? Just one more question. Ah. The bar is dark. You're in da boy. Sometimes we become our surroundings, depending what we surround ourselves wit. So when da boy enters da bar, he finds the absence of light, till she brings her light in. He sees what he missed. Now, the poor son of a bitch can never leave, because he is waiting. He becomes da bar and the bar becomes him.

WALKEN: Or vice versaaa. That son of a bitch was better off in darkness.

COLUMBO: Maybe he just drinks till it closes, ya know what I mean? To close something out of his mind. We all gots something to get out of our brains der.

WALKEN: Are you pla-ying with poop old ma-n?

COLUMBO: It's dirt.

WALKEN: How ca-n you be su-re?

COLUMBO: Who?

At that moment the groans from you, the audience, are unbearable. Tony Kushner, Eric Bogosian, Michael Jackson and Neil Simon, the writers, are in the wings. They stand up to halt this retarded boat wreck opera.

A tussle ensues onstage. It's a bonafide melee. Simon is dead from disconnecting his life support. Kushner is some kind of angelic ninja with pink triangular throwing stars. Michael Jackson is just shadowboxing and that is cool.

Bogosian grabs Walken in a half-nelson and says things you might hear in an action movie, like:

Feel the fever bitch! You deface my play, you
face death. You look hungry. You need a ham sandwich!

Michael Jackson says:

You mean knuckle sandwich, my Buddy. Did my baby walk away? I was boxin'.

I yell out:

I WANT OUT!

Vawoosh.

The theatre goes black. No more heartbeat. Mr. Jackson retreats. With every step he takes, a patch of ground lights up that leads the way out of the nightmare, very similar to the Billie Jean video. The theater patrons follow him out the doors that are, of course, shaped like a vagina and instead of exit at the top it says Happy Birthday. Isn't that nice?

Remorph.

Back to the real bar. Real time. The Red Room. All that stuff Columbo taught me about true strength and inner peace dies the moment I see you.
The humans want to be touched.
He's got you.
And so begins the war of the haves and
the have-nots.
You must not get me wrong. I am not the brokenhearted cliché.
I am the cliché of the critic who can't hide his jealousy.

You both smell like hotel soap. White soap. Stiff towels. Didn't even unfold the v shape on the toilet paper.

In comes chaos theory. You smartypants know what that is.
One small thing affects other things, dollface. How could you ignore this?

I am dealing with you and him in an adult manner.
I think it's time I blew up your night with a warm greeting.

As I approach you are leaning over to him and flirting saying:

I like my movies like I like my men...long and confusing.

That's my cue.
I greet you.
I greet him.
I drop my keys.
I drop my keys so I can spit on his shoes.
I miss.

Not everyone is built for success.
Some are built to get close to winning and
sometimes that feels like winning so ha ha! Goodnight lovebirds. Go get the
worm.

Your shoes have paint on them. You have been painting vigorously. You would
paint your shoes instead of buying new ones. I liked that. We were poor. Our
clothes were old. This paint is new like your tennis bracelet. I coulda made one
for you. I could learn to forge metal. It can't be that hard.

I back off. He's kissing you like you were free sushi. Please be decent.
There was a time when I held you so tight I thought I was alone. We made love
in the strangest season and in the morning you said:

Thank you for the night.

As if I owned it. You made me feel like I did. I felt like handing it over to you.

I thought of things that take apart things.
Tweezers, screwdriver, crowbars and such.
I began breathing hard.

I have made my way out to the parking lot. It seems like I can never get out
here. As if I had been inside this bar since I was a boy. I write you a letter and post it
on the telephone pole above all the other lost animals.

It said:

dear blank and gray shape—
let me come to your wedding.
I'll bring the bouquet.
It will be made out of lead
which is insanely more apropos.
Down the aisle
when you hold it close to your heart
you'll feel something heavy

and when you toss it at the reception
over the junglesnow of your dress
instead of people struggling to reach for the symbol
of falling in love next
they will run
for it will come down on them
like shrapnel fleschettes.

and it will nail some of your relatives in their heads
and they will fall unconscious
and wake up and forget who they are
and I'll be standing there dressed in a rented cupid costume
saying this is love. you're bleeding. walk it off, sissies.

Hot damn. I knew love once. It was my savior.

Sometimes we murder our saviors.

from **HOSTILE PENTECOSTAL**

HOUSTON INTERNATIONAL

*This poem actually happened at the airport in Houston. I smiled like an idiot
the whole plane ride home from my father's house. (Emu poem) I was so amazed, with
all the weirdos out there, that someone would let their kids smooch a total stranger. I'm
glad they did.*

Two nine-year-old girls ran up to me
when I was sitting in the airport,
gave me kisses on my cheeks,
sandwiched me
and ran back to their parents.

Tiny mercenaries.

I watched them giggle.
They 'got me' and asked no questions.
Awkwardly shaped girls giggle hard and red-faced.

They re-circulate the air in my plane and it is torture.
Someone is wearing my lover's old perfume and it hits me every three minutes.
I ask the stewardess for playing cards, ginger ale and duct tape.
I go to light up in the lavatory,
tape up the doorjamb
and imagine lighting up until my skin soaks up the smoke.
People bang on the door
staining their good breeches.
Good.
They don't understand
how your scent
assassinates the day.

But
Your blasting-cap black-eyed romance
Your belladonna body
Your ineffable lust
is nothing
compared to the unforgettable rush
of a coupla giggling nine-year old-girls.

from **THE JOY MOTEL**

SUGARFREE NATIVITY

This actually happened at my pal Tim Scott's house with Jason Whitton and I doing the sneaking of Jesus.

Since we're on the topic of nativity scenes for your front lawn, I must say that I don't like them. Mannequins don't glow for a reason, cause it's creepy. I like the small, defeatable nativity scenes that fit on a mantel and have no chance of chasing you in dreamland.

My mother prefers a paper plate and green coconut shreds that symbolize grass.

She knows where to get edible green coconut. You get a pamphlet on that kind of stuff when you reach fifty-one years of age. Her scene isn't glory struck in lights and plastic, but rather bright candy. The stuff you look at. The kind that makes kids on Halloween pissed and burning-caca-bag prone.

She turns that unwanted candy into glory. Go ahead, all that crap you bought your mothers, the apron that said Best mom ever, the plaque that said Greatest mother in the world, you can go ahead and take those down now that we have a champion. Her name is Nancy.

It's not just candy to her. It's construction of Biblical history. I would eat this Biblical history as a kid 'cause no one told me there was superglue on the back of each piece but so what? I turned out O.K.

The barn is made of graham crackers. A lemon drop for a star. I don't remember Mary and Joseph. They might have been Almond Joy and Mounds. That's right. I remember they were candy bars cause they looked black and delicious. Plenty of animal crackers balanced in the cream waves of frosting.

She says it's snow and I believe her and I wonder if it snows in Israel.
Then I wonder if Jesus was born in Israel.
Then I remembered that Myrrh was a gift and it was also something Egyptians used to stuff in mummy guts. Merry Christmas.

The three wise men:
a red swirled restaurant mint,
a purple bon-bon
and a yellow gummy bear.

191

She says he's the one bearing gold. Now you know where it comes from.

What puts me in aftershock is that my Mother, the Willy Wonka'd God of this world of meticulous frosting and hidden superglue, has made the baby Jesus, the one in swaddling clothes, whatever those are, out of a Sour Patch Kid and a pink roll of taffy. A pink roll of taffy when everyone knows that blue is for boys and pink is for girls. I told her pastor on her.

How could I do such a thing?
First of all you don't mess with the baby Jesus.

The baby Jesus is important. An Italian lady taught me that.

"Don't touch the baby Jesus!" My friend Tim has a mom and she's Italian. She has a porcelain baby Jesus and whenever we'd go to his house, we would turn it a little on the coffee table and she would come in with terror in her jaw when she radared in on that slight sound of porcelain creeping on glass and say "Who turned the baby Jesus?"

We would all stare at each other confused and dumb until I piped up:
    "Why do you have the baby Jesus turned like that, Mrs. Scott?"
    And she would scream at us "So he can watch the T.V. you morons! Don't touch the baby Jesus!" Tim would say "But this movie is rated R and it's got Bill Murray in it."

"Well, Jesus loves Bill Murray too. Now put Jesus back the way he was. Oh, for the love, I'll do it. Next time, don't touch the baby Jesus. You'll break his little head off. "

And you know what friends, we did break his little head off. Not on purpose. It was a sacrilegious act and I am truly ashamed of it. Grown men and women should know better than to play spin the bottle with the baby Jesus figurine. It seemed like the years of backsliding, murder and all-out sin that followed were all a part of some prophecy. Learn from this tale my friends. Never, ever, ever mess with the baby Jesus.

YOU CAN FEEL NEEDED IN A CASINO WITH ONLY A HUNDRED-POUND BAG OF SODIUM-FREE PRETZELS

This was originally called Pechanga and was written for the talented Los Angeles writer Ellyn Maybe. She wears a lot of purple and tape-records every poetry show she goes to and then doesn't label the cassettes and loses them. I think she is fantastic. She loves Billy Jack and vinyl records. I could imagine her detonating a casino from just stepping inside and being wonderful.

The Pechanga casino is a bright blue shoebox
full of Thursday night bingo boots
bawdy belt-buckled cowboys
and heavy alliteration.

Here are the new cowboys:
whoreless
sober
and filtered lights
suburbanites surrounded by neon
spilling across the slots
careful to not kick up dirt from the parking lot.

Indoorsmen.
Overweight.
Charming and unloved.

Rows and Rows of them.
Rub-cuss-begging the prom queen shine machines.

Silver New Mexican turquoise belt buckles
tink-tapping the rims of the chrome slot trays.
A Morse code beggin' for cash mercy.

I pulled up in a dirty Honda,
full of trash and a 100-pound bag of sodium-free pretzels.
It's true. They were a gift.

I merge to blackjack.

The dealer's breath is dead children and boxed wine.
A table littered in flipped rainbow chips.
the colors change in the dealer's mood ring
from sorrow to licorice black.

His hands hover above the velvet.
Chips slip through my fingers like the Eucharist.

My chip appears to be lightly vibrating like a dying joy buzzer.

I can feel the hands of all who had held this chip before me:

The soft hands of a bored policeman,
The sweat in an alcoholic's fingers,
The slice in an elderly woman's golf grip.

I hit and I fold more than an origami factory.
Every hand lost.

Dealer says:
Pechanga wasn't build on nickel slots and winners.
Maybe its not such a good idea to hit on 20.

I make my lame stand.

"What in the name of the Great Spirit
is up with this bum-ass table?"

A bomb of silence
like an anti-Semitic joke in Canter's Deli.

The manager screamed:
"Big Shoe. Airplane Noise. Get him!"

I leeched my body around the Big Bertha five-dollar slot and bellied:
"Noo! I am a quarter Choctaw. We made fancy baskets.
I deserve a cut of your profits and I am not leaving 'til I get it!"

"Get him out of here. He's not even wearing boots."

I chanted Pine Ridge and that I belong everywhere.

They chanted "Reservations!" Double meaning.

I chanted "Billy Jack will come to avenge me
like Jesus flipping out and turning tables in the temple.
Billy Jack, Billy Jack."

They chanted "Jackpot!"

Then a hush fell over the crowd.

BWWIIZZAP!

An electric snap surged through the ground.
Something moved under the trailer.
A hum began to stir upon the velvet tables,
a buzzing like the one I felt in my single chip.

The rum-and-new-carpet odor began to dissipate.
The smell of cooked earth rising.
Glimmer static and drum rolls.

In every machine,
in the pocket of every cowboy and pit boss,
the chips began to murmur,
Richter shake and crawl.

A sound like Hefty bags of teeth on vibrating hotel beds
was growing louder and louder.

Then the chips zipped and burst into the air.
Beautiful rainbow tracers
splitting from tight denim pockets
cleaving and ripping light trails from the cashier's tray
melting the bills
shredding the ceiling stucco into sparks
deep into the sky
never stopping
crashing into comets
tearing into satellites
cell phones exploded
and lovers in Riverside kissed under the fireworks.

Among the quiet rubble of the stunned casino
the pit boss smiled at me and said,
"Did you do that?"

I said, "No. I can't cowboy up like that."

"Well, now what are we gonna gamble with?"

I said, "I have some pretzels."

He said, "No thanks. Too much sodium."

Aha.

AMAZING JIM NUMBER NINE AND SEVEN

This is the first poem I ever wrote that I really felt good about, in 1994. I performed in it 1998 at the Austin Music Hall. I have never heard a thousand people stay perfectly still. I also felt like an ass for shaking so hard from being nervous.

I'm 23. She's 25.

When you lay on your back, your voice sounds different.
I feel like a cloud.

Oh. I've made a woman giddy. Talkative. Abierto.

She used to get her hairspray confused with her deodorant.
How supermarket-hygiene-aisle-Braziliant her locks would smell
And how salon-style-sticky her clean American armpits would feel.

I hear her worlds like a toddler
with floaties
bobbling in blue illuminated night pool.

     Sticky...
Uncomfortable but still...
     I could never...
Horse glue...
     Clumsiest bike...

Something about how she could never do this trick
where you throw your kickstand down as you roll to a stop.
She said she fell like a heavy pancake,
like Jenga in slow-mo.

Lips movin' arms goin' throwin' her kickstand down.

At this point I think of a slow hollow sound.

I didn't bring all this home.
Those pop metaphors.
Those Aquanet armpits.
Those kickstand fingers flicking my chest.

I lay inches from beautiful bedhead
Moonshining hair
500,000 filaments burning.

I cannot cuddle with someone's history.
It takes the anonymity away.
Like hearing a magician's real name.
Like seeing a clown without make-up.
Like honest touch.

How can you hold that.
How could these skinny arms hold all that?
All her clumsy history is kicking my ass.

She pinches my elbow skin.
She says, Amazing. There's no nerves there.

I say, Amazing, I can't feel a thing.

What is the name of that perfect nerve
that tells your eyes to shut tight when pain approaches?

Jim.
Amazing Jim, the magician.

Eyes synchronize shut and now I am no longer here.
No longer bobbling and floating.
Steady.   Running.

Running alongside her.
Slowing her down by gripping the back of the banana seat.

Throw your kickstand down... now!

And we fall
We fall together
Over the spokes
And I feel the spokes
I feel 'em.

And for as long as they remain shut
I am seven and she is nine.

I feel like a cloud, she says.

And I know this is true
for I know the terrible things that go on inside of clouds.

That night drags its nails down the wall
and its sounds like...

THIRTEEN PIECES OF ELECTRICAL TAPE

I hate these numbered poems but I still do it every now and then just to keep my poems in The New Yorker. The girl's name wasn't Rebecca. I went on one date with this gal whom I will call Rebecca and nothing happened. Her family called me a few days later to tell me she had tried to kill herself and I had something to do with it. It may sound cold-hearted, but I didn't go to see her in the hospital when they were sewing her up. I thought it was weak. The rest of the poem just came spilling out after I wrote the Rebecca part. This appeared in Junebug Melatonin.

1.
The average amount of spiders
Someone always swallows in their lifetime
is ten.

I am part of a study
To determine the amount of kisses
dogs attempt to steal from us in our sleep
in a lifetime

but you can't know the results until I die.

2.
So as I'm pouring sugar all over this woman's body
She says Ooooo. Nummy nummy.
Pouring sugar all over my tummy. I want more!

And that's when I pull down the blowtorch mask
And holler 'Crème brulee!'

3.
Rebecca, there's something funny about a girl
with dyed black hair
and a scar on each wrist.

I always say 'Hey, you're supposed to put perfume there.'

4.
Those little skirts that are really just shorts
with a flap in the front
just piss me off

It's deceitful and you know it.

5.
The cops are everywhere
and some are wearing uniforms

6.
There will come a night
when the whole world falls asleep
at the same exact moment
and no one will be guarding the banks
or malls
or jewelry shops
and that's a great time
to sneak into the movies.

if you know how to run a projector.

7.
I lay the same piece of electric tape
over every lover's mouth.

It isn't so sticky anymore.

I wish it wasn't losing its ability to stay.

8.
A kid named Hector said to me
Hey, I got a penny in my shoe.
I asked him if that got a little irritating.
He said, No. They're lucky pennies, silly.
That's all I learned from Hector.

9.
So girl.
What do you like to do?
Do? Um, I dunno. Second base, maybe third.
I meant what do you like to here in Long Beach?
Oh. You mean... Oh. Third base.

10.
Mass confusion
might have something to do with Catholicism.

11.
A man buried his imagination yesterday.

I understood why but disagreed.
He said who can sleep
when imagining clearly those final poses,
that infinite stillness?

I need to sleep.

12.
You will not be detected by aircraft radar. Guaranteed.

13.
My Russian jewel.
These hands turn to Sue Bee honey
and my nails flip to reveal pink crescent moons
when I think of our first night together.

Will it be like a tornado of sheets?
or timed with the cadence of drooling candles
and the bass of pile drivers?

Wild enough to embarrass the furniture.

Woman girl, I want to hold you
the way grasshoppers h
old onto their bows.
The way Russia holds all the sad diamonds.
The way sand creatures hold down sailors' bodies.
The way children hold onto pennies and secrets.

Is it fair to say I might not want to make love on honeymoon night?
Because I might be sore from doing it with you all day
in the train,
under the reception table,
dangling from the helicopter skid like a stuntman from the Kama Sutra,
and in every public restroom we stop at from here
throughout all of North America
cause I'm kinda romantic.

So instead,
that night,
we'll just have to sit there.
Speak about all the pieces of electrical tape
we ever slept with
and wish we had never touched anyone else.

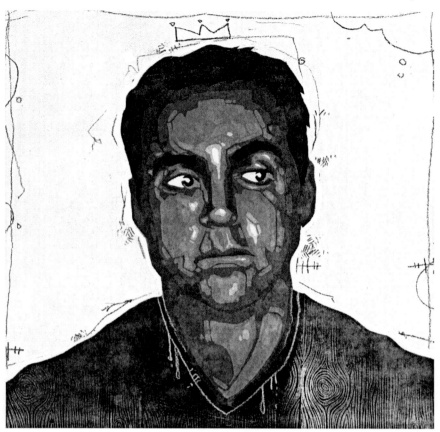

A POET IN PIECES

Derrick Brown was a paratrooper for the 82nd Airborne. He is ordained to perform weddings. He has been published in 4 countries and has won various international writing awards for his poetry. He was a gondolier in Long Beach, CA, a weatherman in Flagstaff, a magician in California and now lives outside of Nashville Tennessee. He tours the world performing his poems. He writes children's books and likes to shoot beer cans with a bow and arrow.